Run, Eunice

Until September 1, 1990 the address
of Ana Publications is

    4343 Garfield Street N. W.
    Washington, D. C. 20007

Run, Eunice

A story of childhood in the 1890s
Clarke County, Alabama

Kathleen White Schad

Ana Publications, Washington, D.C.

© copyright 1990 by Ted Schad

ISBN 0-9618941-1-3

Library of Congress Catalog Card Number 90-082162

Printed in the United States of America

Published by Ana Publications
4427 Westover Place, N.W.
Washington, D.C. 20016
(202) 362-5330

Cover illustration by Robert C. Rooney

All rights reserved.

Contents

Foreword vii
Editor's Preface ix
Author's Note x
The Griffin Family xi

1 School 1
2 Christmas Time 9
3 Sister Mattie 15
4 At Aunt Lyddie's 25
5 The Preachers 35
6 The Preachers' Return 43
7 The Ugly Stage 49
8 The Wedding 55
9 Pastimes 65
10 Tin Peddler 73
11 Playing Lady at Grandma Holland's 85
12 A Squirrel, a Catfish, and the Whip 93
13 Molasses Making 103
14 Halloween 109
15 Eunice Grows Up 115

Historical Note 131

Foreword

Run, Eunice is a gem for readers of all ages. A blend of fiction, history, and Americana, it has the quality of literature. Essentially, it is the story of bright and sensitive Eunice Griffin, growing up at the turn of the century, in a family of eleven brothers and sisters. Older siblings are called, out of customary respect for seniority, Sister Mattie, Sister Mary, Brother Ellis, and so forth. By the end of the story, Eunice has become Sister Eunice to her younger brother, Boland.

There are intimate, detailed descriptions of southern country life. The one-room schoolhouse was built of boards "a foot wide and twelve feet long. A bench ran around the wall so that sixty-five children could sit on it and lean back against the wall." There is a chapter on the process and excitement of making molasses. The Griffins milk cows and churn butter, sew a wedding dress and hold an "infare." They own and care for animals, including a pet goat and squirrel, and one fine horse, Midnight. "Midnight represented Papa's every earthly weakness. Papa realized it, too." Food is produced and prepared with something like reverence.

The pastimes of country children are wonderful to read. Sliding on barrel staves down hills covered in pine straw, swinging on muscadine vines, fishing. But when Eunice and Boland abandon five fishes on a stump, Eunice gets a switching with a peach-tree switch by Papa. "What's gotten into you, Eunice? You don't leave fish on a stump. Either leave them in the creek to live, or bring them home to eat. The idea of taking those fish out of water and leaving them to die or be wasted!"

While Papa switches, Mama hides in the kitchen. She feels obliged to hold still since she can never bring herself "to undertake any punishment at all."

What admirable, lovable people! I hope this book will be read and loved as it deserves, that it will live forever.

Mary Ward Brown
Winner of the
PEN/Hemingway Award 1987
for *Tongues of Flame*

Editor's Preface

Kathleen (Kay) White Schad was born in Aliceville, Alabama, the sixth child of Eunice Griffin and George Bryant White. The White family moved to Canton, Mississippi, in 1924, where Kay attended the public schools, graduating from Canton High School in 1935. She then attended Judson College in Marion, Alabama, from which she received her A.B. degree in 1939. Over the next four years she served as librarian at Judson and taught French while earning a degree in library science from the Louisiana State University summer school.

In 1943 she moved to Seattle, Washington, where she married Ted Schad. After coming to Washington, D.C., in 1946, she worked in the Schools Division of the D.C. Public Library and subsequently in the Navy Department Library, from which she resigned in 1955 to raise her two daughters, Mary Jane and Rebecca.

This book is based on Kay's mother's reminiscences of her childhood on a farm near Thomasville, Alabama, in the 1890s, as told to Kay over the years. Kay died in August 1989, leaving the manuscript of the book, which she had been unable to complete because of the ravages of the brain tumor which ended her life. Final editing and publication of the book was undertaken by Ted in appreciation for fifty wonderful years of friendship and love with Kay.

Ted Schad

Author's Note

Every mother has more than one childhood. One is the actual. The others are each of her children's visualizations of it. Eunice was my mother. The book paints a picture of the place and the time and the customs of her childhood, based on my mother's recollections, told to me during the years that I was growing up and when I came home for visits after I was married. But the people, even Eunice, and most of the events are only my visualization of them.

Kathleen White Schad

The Griffin Family
Clarke County, Alabama, 1892

Ivey Griffin—Papa
Lou Holland Griffin—Mama
Bud Nap—grown and living away from home
Bud (Horrie)—grown and living away from home
Sister Maggie—grown and living away from home
Sister Mattie
Sister Mary
Sister Nora
Brother Ellis
Brother Bunyan
Brother Fowler
Eunice
Boland

 *one*

School

"Run, Eunice, and get Bo's slate. It'll be a lot faster for you to go than for us to wait for Bo to go get it himself."

Eunice Griffin hurried back into the house to fetch her little brother Boland's slate which he had neglected to bring. Pokey little Bo. This was his first year in school, and he hadn't yet learned how to hurry.

Out at the gate waiting with Bo were their older brothers and sisters who were still of school age: Sister Mary, Sister Nora, Brother Ellis, Brother Bunyan, Brother Fowler. Sister Mary, the oldest, was now seventeen; Sister Nora was sixteen. The boys, also a year apart, ranged down to Brother Fowler who was thirteen.

"Here come the Days!" shouted Bo.

The children of the Day family rounded the bend in the road and quickened step to join them. Eunice came skipping back with Bo's slate in time to walk with Alice Day.

"Oh, Eunice," Alice sighed, "You are lucky. We've already walked more than a mile before you even have to start. I do believe ours is the dustiest part."

She looked down at her bare feet now red from the clay dust. It was summer, and none of them wore shoes. Eunice thought a while. "Yes, but we have to walk to your place and back in the evenings to get the mail, so what's the difference?"

1

The Days' father owned a sawmill, gin, and store with the post office in it over at Glover in the opposite direction from school.

School was held in the summer because the farms were not so busy during those months. Many children missed school in the spring to help plow, plant, and hoe, and again in the fall to help pick the cotton, dig the potatoes, pull the corn, and cut the cane. A three-month summer session was held so that those children might catch up. But Papa and Mr. Day had wage-hands and sent their children to school all twelve months of the year.

Alice and Eunice began gathering wild pink and white phlox as they walked along. It would look so pretty in a jar on the teacher's table. Boland lagged behind.

"Hooooo-ooooooo. Hooooooo-ooooooooooooooo. Won't wait for me."

All the other children stopped and waited. But as soon as they stopped, Bo stopped. He wouldn't budge an inch. He just stood there wailing, "Hooooooo-ooooooooooo."

Brother Ellis stamped his foot. "That young'un. Why do we have to put up with this every morning? He's done it every day since he started to school."

"Hooooooo-ooooooo. Hooooooo-ooooooooooooooo."

From across the pastures and on top of the hill opposite the Griffin's place came an echo, "Hooooooo-ooooooooooo. Hooooooooo-ooooooooooo."

That was Frank Walker who lived with his grandfather over there. He was mocking Boland.

By then the older children had retraced their steps to Bo. "Shame on you. Hear Frank making fun of you?"

Eunice chided him. "Bo, I carry your speller for you. Next thing you'll expect me to carry you, too."

Down the road a piece Newell Williams and her younger brother, Carlos, were waiting at their gate to join them. Carlos was a beginner like Bo.

Newell took over. "Now, listen, Carlos. You and Bo walk ahead of us, and Alice, Eunice, and I promise to stay behind you. That way Bo can't say we won't wait for him."

The older Days and Griffins, freed at last, were soon out of sight. Eunice, Alice, and Newell had to watch their feet constantly to keep from stepping on Bo's heels. They began to while away the tedious walk by talking about doll clothes.

"Sister Mary and Sister Nora look at those patterns in the *Delineator* and want every dress they see. Sister Mary's just made herself a new blue pongee and Sister Nora's working on a yellow organdy. I think there are enough scraps left to make dresses for my little doll and yours, too."

Newell was pleased. "That would be wonderful. Nobody has as many scraps as you, Eunice. Your Sister Mary and your Grandma Holland sew more 'n anybody else in Clarke County."

"I deserve scraps," sighed Eunice. "Think of all the hours I spend turning the pedal on that old Wheeler and Wilson machine for Sister Mary. It's so heavy she can't sew very long unless I sit on the floor behind it and push the bar between the treadle and the wheel for her. She says, "I sew for you, and you have to pedal for me." I practically memorize those *Delineator* magazines while I wait between turns."

They had barely reached the school yard when Eunice felt someone yank her braids. She looked around. It was Omer Griffin, one of her Uncle John's boys. As she climbed the steps, she felt his toes on her heels. He yanked her braids again as they entered the schoolhouse. She wheeled and looked at him in silent indignation. It was mean to pick on her in school where she had to be quiet.

The schoolhouse was built of rough boards a foot wide and twelve feet long. Like most rural Alabama buildings in 1892, it was unpainted. Oh, a few rich folks had painted houses, but nobody else.

Inside, the schoolhouse was just one large room. A bench ran around the wall so that the sixty-five children could sit on it and lean back against the wall. The wood-burning stove and a chair and table for the teacher were the only other furnishings. In winter the boys had to spend their recess time chopping wood for the stove, but now that summer was here there was no need for it.

As Eunice took her place on the bench, she noticed that the hole which had been in the chimney a long time had grown larger. A good thing it was summer. The mud and straw had just dropped away, and you could see right outdoors through it.

Mr. Kimbrough rapped the class to order. Eunice looked at his pleasant face and thought, "I would like him a lot if he didn't act as if he'd like to marry Sister Mattie and take her away."

Sister Mattie was at home. She was eighteen now and no longer a school pupil with the rest of them. Eunice loved her best of all. She sat thinking of Mattie's gentle round face and kindly, big blue eyes. Nora was supposed to be the prettiest in the family, but Eunice thought Mattie much prettier. Never had she seen harshness on Mattie's face. Sister Mary and Sister Nora were always shrieking with laughter and fun to be with, but they were sharp tongued when she did wrong. Sister Mattie had never said one cross word to her in her life, no matter what mistakes she made.

Mr. Kimbrough was calling the roll. My, there were a lot of Griffins when you counted in Eunice's brothers and sisters and cousins. Most answered, "Present."

Some of the more ambitious ones answered with verses or lines from the scriptures. Brother Bunyan's was, "Be ye doers of the word and not hearers only." Brother Ellis gave his favorite about David, "His strength was as the strength of ten because his heart was pure." Little Cousin Fannie said,

"Twinkle, twinkle little star, How I wonder what you are."
Eunice was still thinking about Sister Mattie. She chose the beautiful line from the story of David and Jonathan. "He loved him as he loved his own soul."
Soon the drone of recitations filled the warm morning air. But it was no time before the lessons were punctuated by grunts. Pigs! There were snouts poling into the hole in the chimney. Oink! Oink! Oink! The grunts were especially loud as they echoed in the chimney.
There were a few pieces of stove wood left from winter. Mr. Kimbrough picked up one and poked it at the snouts, saying, "Go away, pigs. Go away."
But the pigs persisted. Poor Mr. Kimbrough. Sixty-five children of all ages and now four pigs. The children were rolling and shrieking with delight.
Three of the pigs finally became convinced that there was no food to be found there and wandered on. Then lessons were resumed in the McGuffey readers until noon.

When school was dismissed for dinner, Eunice and Bo and their older brothers and sisters met the children of their Uncle John Griffin at a long table out under the trees. As they gathered around, a wage-hand from home and one from Uncle John's farm rode up on mules. Dangling on one side of each mule was a large basket of hot dinner and on the other a long tin cooler of buttermilk, which had been hanging in the well all morning.
In the spring and fall the children brought cold lunches, but in midsummer the farms were not as busy so somebody could

be spared to bring part of the dinner that was being served at home.

Today the Ivey Griffin children had chicken dumplings, corn bread, string beans, corn on the cob, beets, onions, hot green peppers, and a big peach pie. Uncle John's gang had almost the same thing though their chicken was fried and their pie was double-crust apple.

On Eunice's left was Cousin Omer. He tried to sneak a piece of hot green pepper into Brother Ellis's string beans.

"Omer!" Brother Ellis protested. "I see what you're up to. Keep your hands away from my plate!"

In a minute or two Omer was reaching around Ellis's back, trying to slip some of the pepper into cousin Lily's beets. She caught him and slapped his hand. "Behave, Omer," she pled.

Omer seemed to quiet down as he finished his big square of corn bread. Then he leaned toward Eunice, "Look here, Coot!"

Brother Fowler had called her that disgusting name once, and Omer had seized upon it and kept it up. She turned toward him. She had no idea what it meant, but she was sure it was something unpleasant.

Just then Omer took up a pod of hot pepper. He seized Eunice firmly and rubbed it hard into every inch of her face. He did it so fast that she was not even sure what he was doing until the pepper began to burn.

Her fair thin skin felt as though it were being broiled. Her eyes were on fire. Screaming, she jumped up and ran back and forth wildly. But she could not escape the searing heat by running because it was on her face; it was rubbed into her face. Never had Eunice felt such pain. Even thoughtless Omer was contrite when he saw how she was suffering.

"Oh, Eunice, I didn't know it would be so awful. I wouldn't have done it if I'd'a known it'd be that bad."

Sister Nora had an inspiration. "Give me that butter!" She

snatched up the mound of soft sweet butter and began plastering it all over Eunice's face. Oh, but it felt soothing to Eunice. Nothing could really stop the burn, but it was nice to have somebody try to help her.

By the time Mr. Kimbrough rang the bell for the afternoon session, Eunice could endure standing still, but the steady, slow burn continued. She was an arresting sight. Normally Eunice appeared to be a slight little girl whose tow hair worn in two pigtails framed eyes of a deep and brilliant blue. But today her eyes were eclipsed by her flaming, glistening skin. As the butter melted, it began trickling down her neck. Her braids were sodden with it, and big greasy blotches of it were all over her best pinafore. Newell stood off and looked at her as though paralyzed in silent alarm.

When Mr. Kimbrough caught sight of her, Sister Nora explained what had happened. He shook his head.

"My, Eunice, you look a sorry mess. I think you had better be excused for this afternoon. Miss Nora, I'll excuse you, too, to walk home with your sister."

Nora gathered up their books, and they set out.

As their feet sank to the ankles in the hot red dust on the road home, Eunice wept again. "Sister Nora, those mean boys like Omer pick on me more than anybody, don't they?"

"Indeed, they seem to, Eunice. I think you're going to have to learn to take up for yourself. You're just going to have to *show* them, you hear me?"

Eunice resolved to talk it over further with Sister Mattie after supper. Papa was out in the field and was the first to see them coming. He called out, "Why, what's happened to you, Ootchie?"

Ootchie. That was second only to *Coot.* Here she had to call all the older ones Sister and Brother in order to show proper respect for her elders. But did anybody call her Sister Eunice? No. Not even Boland.

 *two*

Christmas Time

Summer gradually cooled into fall, but not until the second week of December was the weather really cold. Papa and the boys started preparations for hog killing, and at the same time Mama and Sister Mattie, Sister Mary, and Sister Nora began the Christmas baking.

It was: "Run, Eunice. Bring me three eggs."

"Eunice, run. Take this cup and fill it to the rim with sugar. And don't spill."

"Run, Eunice. Get a bowl of butter from the safe."

They didn't let her help make the cakes at all. She was only allowed to do the running. The closest she came to real participation was when Sister Mattie said, "Here, Eunice. You may flour the raisins for this fruitcake."

Day after day the Christmas baking went on. They baked pies: coconut cream and potato custard. They baked little tea cakes. And cakes, oh my: fruitcake, loaf cake, marble cake, jelly cake, silver and gold cake, spice cake, chocolate cake, molasses cake, pound cake, great white cakes covered with fluffy icing and grated fresh coconut.

The oven in the stove out in the shed room could not hold so many cakes at a time, but it did not matter. Sister Mattie brought her big fruit cake out to the fireplace in the dining room. A big iron skillet on three legs nestled in the embers. She lifted the lid and set the pan containing the cake batter down into the skillet. Then she replaced the skillet lid and brushed hot coals on top of it.

"There. That'll make a perfect slow oven for this fruit cake."

The best part of the baking season in Eunice's and Boland's eyes was the bowls and platters to be licked. Today Sister Nora was icing the last chocolate cake. Eunice bribed Bo. "Bo, let me lick just this one chocolate icing. You've had them all today. I just had that little bit left from the coconut cake. There was hardly any in that one."

"Naw."

"*Please.*"

"Naw."

Sister Mary laughed. "Eunice, you needn't worry. He drank all the milk out of the coconuts, and he's licked at least four bowls this evening. He's bound to give out soon."

"Please, Bo."

"Naw."

Sister Nora gave the chocolate cake a final examination before abandoning the icing bowl. "There. Looks delicious, doesn't it? Well, here's the bowl to lick."

Eunice elbowed in. She had had very little icing today, and this was her last chance. She bent over the bowl and encircled it with both arms. Then she began greedily scraping it with a spoon. Bo began pushing her and clamoring, "Now, give me some. I want some. Move over and let me have some."

Just then Papa opened the door. Eunice's face was buried in the bowl and he could see only the crown of her tow-head. The top edge of the bowl was completely immured by her arms. Bo, wailing piteously, immediately appealed to him. "Hooooooo-oooooooo! Papa, Eunice won't let me have a taste!"

Papa reached up to the mantel piece and snatched down one of the peach-tree switches. No switch was more cutting than those off the peach trees, and he always kept a few back in the shadows on the high mantelpieces. "In my life I have never seen a more selfish sight. Eunice! Aren't you ashamed to be such a pig? The very idea of treating your little brother this way. I am surprised at you!"

As Papa advanced with the switch, Eunice indignantly lifted her head from the bowl. Just then Mama bobbed in the kitchen door and immediately disappeared again. She could not bear to punish a child herself nor could she watch when Papa whipped. Because she renounced all responsibility for discipline, she never felt free to interfere in any way. Papa sighed at Eunice's willfulness and raised the switch.

But Sister Mattie dropped a lid with a clatter and came hurtling breathlessly across the room. She stayed his hand in mid-air.

"No, Papa! Oh, no. You don't understand. You were not here. Boland is the one who's a pig. He's had four big icing bowls and he drank every drop of the coconut milk. Eunice barely had a taste today until just now. Boland won't even let her lick this one bowl in peace. For goodness sake, don't switch *her*."

Papa promptly put the switch back up on the mantelpiece. To Boland he turned and said sternly, "Boland, quit aggravating Eunice. Just stand back and leave her alone. And not another whine out of you."

"Sister Mattie, I wish you'd look after me the way you do Eunice," Brother Fowler grumbled as he deposited a load of stove wood by the fireplace. "Nobody pays any attention to my interests. Fifteen cakes and not a fallen one in the lot. Far as I'm concerned, they're not much good unless they fall. *When* is one of you going to make me a sad cake?"

Mama emerged from the kitchen corner with a peal of laughter. "Oh, Fowler! I guess you'll have to make one yourself and bang the oven door shut. That's supposed to make them fall."

Beaming and relieved, she began tying on a fresh apron. It was a beautiful one, cross-stitched in a morning glory design. Nobody was daintier than Mama, always in a stiff clean apron made glorious with ruffles and embroidery and tied in back with a generous bow. With an air of sweeping out the squabbling, tears, and rebukes so abhorrent to her, she proposed gaily, "Let's make the taffy today. That would be fun, wouldn't it? Run, Eunice. Get two gallons of molasses so we'll have an extra gallon for taffy."

It was Eunice's regular job to keep the dining table supplied with molasses. Once a week she took a gallon-sized stone pitcher out to the smokehouse where it was stored. Today she put on her cloak because of the cold and drizzle outside.

The barrels of molasses rested on a bench. There was a faucet near the bottom of the barrels from which Eunice drew the mahogany colored ribbon-cane molasses. It was thick and slow to run. She had to wait and wait. Her toes got so cold that she jumped from foot to foot, and she rubbed her hands together to warm them. The smokehouse was gloomy and dark. Above her hung the meat, smelling pungently of salt and hickory smoke.

She picked up a straw and poked it down in a hole in the dirt floor. "Doodlebug, doodlebug, come out of your hole." She drew up the straw with a jerk. No bug. She spat in the dirt and muddied the straw. The bug would surely stick to the wet mud. She put in the straw and pulled it up once more. Still no luck. She tried again and again. No luck.

When the pitchers were finally filled with molasses, she hastily delivered one to Mama and then ran back again to fetch the second.

It was good to get back to the cozy kitchen building. Mama had already put the first gallon of molasses on the stove to boil.

"Oh, my, Eunice, that Major slipped in behind you when you came in."

Major was the little new puppy. The bustle of the Christmas cooking delighted him. He scampered happily around all those feet and nuzzled Sister Nora as she poured out the cooked molasses into buttered platters to cool. She warned, "Major! Be careful or you'll be a candied puppy!"

Sister Mattie soon motioned to Eunice, "I think that by the time we butter our hands it'll be cool enough for us to start pulling."

Eunice and Mattie gingerly picked up a great piece of cooked molasses and began to pull it back and forth between them. Gradually the dark taffy lightened into a sparkling golden color. Eunice sighed with pleasure. The taffy would be good to eat, but pulling it with Sister Mattie was the best part of all.

❀ *three*

Sister Mattie

The week after Christmas was a whirl of pound suppers for the young folks. Sister Mary and Sister Nora didn't always go with the same young man, but this year Mr. Kimbrough called for Sister Mattie every evening.

It was disheartening day after day to watch the three girls open up the big lard cans where the cakes were stored and take so much out to carry off to the suppers. Off Mattie had gone this time with half a great white coconut cake. Mary took chocolate and Nora took silver and gold.

"Just one little piece off it," Bo begged Nora.

"The idea! You're not starving. Mama's got cake." But somehow the cake the older ones were taking away looked better than the cake left at home.

The three big boys were going to the supper tonight on Papa's two horses and a mule. Bo and Eunice glowered. There was Brother Fowler proudly sitting up on the mule. Thirteen years old now, and could go to the fruit suppers this year. He was carrying nuts to the party: butternuts and pecans. Only once a year did Papa buy nuts. It seemed unforgivable for Fowler to take any away.

Brother Bunyan acted like a veteran. He was fourteen and had been to some suppers last year. A sack of raisins bulged out of the pocket of his cloak. Why, there were more raisins in that bag than Bo and Eunice got in their stockings in two or three Christmases! Surely he didn't have to have *that* many.

But the one they envied and resented most was Brother Ellis. He was fifteen, the oldest boy at home, and he was the only one Papa allowed to ride Midnight.

Midnight. Eunice held her breath as Ellis led her from her stall. Midnight was so beautiful that everybody around this part of the country just stood still and looked when she came in sight. There was not one light hair on her. She was black: a liquid, glistening black. Midnight did not belong on a farm like the Griffins'. She was their unlikely possession due to Papa's friendship with Jasper Jarvis. Mr. Jarvis had made a trip with Papa down to Mobile to buy a horse. They got down there and saw Midnight and lost their senses. Especially Mr. Jarvis. As soon as he saw her he couldn't be satisfied with any of the others. He was determined that Papa should have her, and Papa could not resist. She had cost so much money that to this day Papa had never admitted to anybody else what he paid. He was ashamed. Not even one good milk cow on his farm and him buying a horse like that.

Oh, my, how he did take on over that horse. He and Brother Ellis spent hours feeding her the best of everything, currying and brushing her, and polishing her saddle.

Not only was Ellis being allowed to ride Midnight to the suppers, he was carrying oranges. Right out in a string bag where you could see them. Six great big oranges. Mama did make cake all during the year, but butternuts, pecans, raisins, and oranges they waited for from one Christmas until the next.

Eunice and Bo could not bear it. As Ellis rode up on Midnight, they charged, one on each side of him, and began pounding his legs with their fists. "Give us an orange! Give us an orange! Just one! Just one to divide! You're getting to ride Midnight and you're taking off the oranges, too. Not fair, not fair, not fair!"

Mama had to run out and stop them. "Hush, Eunice! Hush, Boland! Don't you realize you may excite Midnight and get hurt? Now, you two leave Ellis alone. It's expected that a boy his age bring fruit, and a half-dozen oranges is none too many. He's practically a young man now. Behave yourselves and stand back here."

Eunice and Bo could only stand back and watch them go out the gate. First solemn little Fowler on his tacky mule. Then jolly Bunyan on plain Ben. And then Ellis on Midnight, as handsome a pair as you ever saw.

Ellis was slender, all smiles, and his guitar was slung 'round his shoulder. Somehow Ellis would have belonged on Midnight even if he had not been the oldest. He was the fox hunter. The other boys didn't care about hunting anything more exciting than coons or possums, but Ellis could not be satisfied with that. He'd say, "It's music to hear those hounds baying a fox. It's the prettiest music in the world."

As the boys rode out of sight Eunice complained, "I don't see why I can't go. I'm about as old as Brother Fowler."

"Yes, but this is the first year he's gone. And he's a boy. Boys get out sooner than girls. Your turn will come."

Another two years to wait. Or, more likely, three or four years.

Eunice and Bo filled the late afternoon by caring for their pets. Bo found some scraps for the puppy, Major, and Eunice watered her pet nanny goat, which her Grandpa Holland had given her. She gave Nanny a brief lecture while she drank: "Listen, Nanny. You quit eating up everything you can find. Folks around here are fussing about how you eat up clothes. Nobody has any to spare. They don't complain to you, but they keep telling me they're not going to stand for it. They say I'll have to get rid of you."

The December days were so short that darkness soon began to settle, and the farm seemed deserted and cheerless. There was nobody with Eunice at supper that night but Mama, Papa, Bo, a lightning-rod agent who had sought shelter for the night, and the wage-hands, Cephas and Felix, whose house was in the back. Felix was not really a hand because he was only twelve. But he lived in the house with Cephas and helped out with light chores.

The lightning-rod agent was a young man named Mr. Dunning. He had spent the night with them once before. Tonight he looked up and down the table, gulped, and asked wistfully, "Uh. Miss Mattie? Uh. Miss Mary? Uh. Miss Nora? And, uh. The boys?"

Mama understood his disappointment and explained gently, "They're all at a pound supper tonight. All six of them."

Mr. Dunning sighed. He had tired himself to travel this far so that he might ask for shelter at the Griffins' where there were three such gay and pretty daughters. Everybody did; he was not at all an unusual visitor. There was nearly always somebody extra: traveling photographers, picture-enlargers, peddlers in covered wagons or with packs on their backs, drummers, wrought-iron range salesmen, sheriffs and deputy sheriffs, relatives, and friends of relatives. The dining table was always banked with food in anticipation, and the cribs across the road always held more than enough for the visitors' horses.

Boland looked up and grinned mischievously. "Yes, sirree, this is one night I'm going to sleep on the bed!"

"Boland!" Papa and Mama admonished.

Then they all laughed together, and Mr. Dunning volunteered, "Well, now that you mention it, Boland, I do recall that you and your next older brother did have to put a mattress on the floor the last time I was here. That *is* so."

Since each bed in the house had a feather mattress on top of a cotton mattress on top of a grass mattress, it was simple to make room for company; they just slipped out the cotton mattress and threw it on the floor. The company slept on the bed, and the younger children slept on the floor.

"We have to make down the bed nearly every night," blurted out Bo.

Bo was letting out a standing family complaint and joke. Papa thought it was sinful to turn anybody away at night. He took them all, even if the family had to sleep on the floor. He allowed no dancing or other foolishness and was strict about eight o'clock bedtime, but, even so, Mattie, Mary, and Nora attracted more than the Griffins' fair share of travelers. Mama, too, gave reason for so many. She was so gracious that she made each one feel as if it were a delight to have him and not one bit of extra bother.

After supper Eunice had to churn. It was tiring to churn without Sister Mattie alongside chatting. Eunice and Mattie usually giggled and talked so much that the butter would come before they thought once of peeking inside. But tonight her arm ached, and she began to look for the butter long, long before it was made. She was glad when she finally finished and could join Papa who was on his way to the house.

Bo and the lightning-rod agent were sitting by the fire peeling and chewing ribbon cane. Papa settled down with the *Alabama Christian Advocate*.

Just then Felix stuck his head in the door and caught her eye. "Yo' Mama want you. Better run."

"Where is she?"

"Still out in the kitchen."

Eunice put on her cloak. The night air was too chilly to get there from the house without a wrap. The kitchen was a good distance from the house. It was built separate because there were fires in both the stove and the fireplace most of the time. If it should burn down, the house was far enough away to be saved unless there was a strong wind. She ran along the raised plank walk and banged in breathlessly. "Yes'm. Here I am."

Mama regarded her with a puzzled look. "My goodness, what are you doing here, Eunice? I told you all that churning was enough for you to do tonight."

"Why, Felix said you wanted me."

"Felix! Ho! That boy and his foolishness." Mama shook her head and laughed. "No, I didn't send for you, Eunice!"

"Again? Mama! He does this to me all the time. Half the time you really want me, and half the time you don't. How can I ever know?"

Mama tried to console her. "Oh, Eunice, you were born into a family of teasers. And, being the youngest girl in such a big family, you are bound to catch a lot of it. Might as well resign yourself."

But Eunice could not resign herself. She was outraged. She left and clattered back down the dark, cold walk. From his house in the back yard Felix called in a mocking voice, "April Fool!"

She stopped and shouted back at him. "It is not April Fool. It's not even New Year's yet. Felix, will you ever learn that April Fool is one day and not every day?"

When she reached Mama's room again Bo and the agent had disappeared. They had grown tired of chewing cane and had gone to bed in the boys' shed room.

My, Mama's room was quiet. Nobody in here now but Papa reading by the lamp and not saying a word. Eunice glanced around her. She loved this great old room. When Mama and Papa got married back before The War, they had started with just a one-room log house. Later as their fortune and the family grew, they had enclosed it as part of a frame house. This room was that original log house. It was far cozier than the rest of the house in winter and much the coolest spot in summer. And it was a big, big room since it used to be the whole house. It held two large poster beds, Papa's great old secretary, a dresser, a washstand, a trunk, Mama's Wheeler and Wilson sewing machine, and up near the fireplace were four rocking chairs and half a dozen straight chairs.

The party was so far away that the company was staying and spending the night. It would be late tomorrow morning before Eunice's older sisters and brothers would be home. She sighed and went on back to the girls' shed room.

The shed room shared the unusual silence. The bed was cold and damp. She was used to sleeping with Sister Mattie. Nora and Mary had always had the bed in the other corner, and when Sister Maggie had married years ago, Eunice had moved in with Sister Mattie. Now she could hardly remember back before that.

She missed Mary and Nora, too. At bedtime they recalled all the funny incidents of the day, and gales of laughter came fitfully from their side of the room. The farther Eunice inched herself down under the covers, the colder the bed felt. She made a small ball of herself, but even so she could not manage to create a warm spot.

Even though he had taken Sister Mattie to the fruit supper every night that week, Mr. Kimbrough came again on Sunday afternoon. He talked to Mama and Papa in the company room. Sister Mattie stayed out back in the dining room.

Eunice was busy swishing the crumbs off the top of the sandy floor with her little grass broom. It was easier to sweep crumbs off sand than to carry water in from the well and scrub the dining room floor. The sand kept the hand-hewn floor beneath it beautifully white and smooth. Sister Mattie seemed to be hunting things to keep her busy. She made Eunice feel uneasy. It didn't seem natural.

Then, just as if she didn't have company up front, Mattie reached up into the safe for her jar full of a dried weed called Life Everlasting. She filled a corncob pipe with it. At this Eunice could not suppress a grin. Oh, but it looked funny to see Mattie, dainty as a doll, sitting there with that messy homemade pipe in her mouth.

Mattie laughed heartily, too, but stopped suddenly as she began to wheeze. It was because she had asthma that she was smoking the Life Everlasting. It always made her feel better. She asked Eunice between puffs, "Where is your pipe?"

Sometimes Eunice and Bo stuck a piece of cane into a hollowed-out end of a corncob and made themselves pipes, too, but today Eunice didn't want to. Today seemed too different. She couldn't remember Mama and Papa ever sitting up in the company room. It was always taken over by the older girls and the young men.

After a long time Mr. Kimbrough, Papa, and Mama emerged. But they didn't say anything special. Their faces were pleasant masks. Sister Mattie joined them and then walked out to the gate with Mr. Kimbrough. All of it so strange, and yet not one of them offering a word of explanation. Eunice hated the pretense. It was like a threatening summer thunderstorm that blackens the sky and makes the air heavy and yet refuses to break.

But actually she had to wait no later than supper time to hear the reason. Papa was not one to harbor mysteries, and once he had the entire family together he came right out with it.

"We may as well tell you all at once. The folks at Choctaw Corner want Mr. Kimbrough to promise to teach there next fall. You know that's where he comes from. Mr. Kimbrough says he'd like to accept if he can take Mattie with him. Your mother and I have promised him that if he and Mattie will wait until next October we'll give our consent to the marriage."

My, such a clamor! Sister Mary and Sister Nora squealed with excitement.

Brother Bunyan began roaring, "Teacher's pet! Teacher's pet!"

Brother Ellis laughed, "I can just see our spelling matches from now on. The words will all be things like L-O-V-E and S-W-E-E-T-H-E-A-R-T. Hoo! Hoo!"

"And H-U-G."

"And K-I-S-S."

Oh, how could they giggle and joke and be so silly? Eunice felt clammy and sick all over. She could not look at Mattie. Didn't Mr. Kimbrough know that Sister Mattie was her partner? Her sleeping partner and her work partner? And Sister Mattie? Surely she knew that getting married meant abandoning her and the rest of the family, too. Why, Bud Nap and Bud and Sister Maggie were married, and she didn't know them any better than lots of people who were no kin. Mattie surely would not willfully be disloyal to her. Love must be something like a terrible spell of malaria that just comes on you and takes you off.

❀ *four*

At Aunt Lyddie's

A horse came clopping down the road pulling a buggy in a cloud of dust. In it was Aunt Lyddie Griffin, Uncle John's wife, on her way home from the store. She decided to stop in for a drink of water from the bucket kept on the shelf at the end of the porch. Then she agreed to sit down with Mama to rock and cool off awhile. As Aunt Lyddie rocked and fanned herself with a big palmetto fan, she noticed Eunice out in the yard piling up grass to make a doll bed. She called out to her, "Eunice, why don't you and Bo come over Saturday and spend the night with my crowd? Grandpa Griffin's with us this week and you'd get to see him, too."

Eunice rejoiced. Nobody was so gay as Uncle John, Aunt Lyddie, and their ten children. Queer thing. Papa had been a merry boy who came back from the Civil War a serious man. But his serious brother John had come back with a light heart. He liked nothing better than crowds of young folks and children with all their noise and foolishness. Strange indeed. Wars just must turn people inside out.

Finally Saturday came. Along about three o'clock Bo asked, "Papa, you going to let Eunice and me ride Midnight to Uncle John's?"

"Not today, Boland. Think you'd better take Old Cap this time."

Papa didn't laugh, and Bo didn't either, though this was a

big joke between them. Actually Bo did not expect to ride Midnight as long as he lived, but he always asked from sheer excitement at the very idea. He knew that he and Eunice were permanently assigned to Old Cap, the laziest mule on the place. Old Cap was too slow to hurt anybody. In fact he was so slow they could hardly make him move at all.

Eunice went out and threw a sack across Old Cap to keep the hairs off her clothes. She and Bo led him up to the raised kitchen walk to mount him, and off they rode. Actually they could have walked down the public road and up the lane to Uncle John's faster. But a mount somehow gave their visit more dignity.

As they turned up Uncle John's lane, Eunice cried, "Look, Bo! Uncle John's peaches look ripe. His are earlier than ours. You can ride Old Cap on up to the house. I'm stopping for peaches."

When Bo reached the house Cousin Lily asked him, "Where's Eunice?"

"She's up in a peach tree eating peaches."

"They're not good ripe yet."

"Eunice starts eating them as soon as they get just a little streak of pink on them."

"Let's go get her before she gets sick."

Lily appeared under the tree and urged Eunice, "Come on. Get down, Eunice. You don't want the stomach ache, do you? You ought to be ashamed. You haven't been up to the house to speak to Grandpa Griffin. Come on—speak to Grandpa, and then let's play hiding."

They could see Grandpa Griffin long before they reached the house. He was in a rocker in the big center hall catching the breeze both ways. But Eunice was dismayed as she drew closer. My, but he seemed feeble. Eunice had heard the family say that he was failing, but even so she felt unprepared. What to say after she had greeted him? What to do?

Lily sensed her discomfort and said firmly, "Remember? We were going to play hiding."

Grandpa waved her on. "Go ahead and play with the others, Eunice, hon."

Hiding was a good game. There were so many good hiding places over here. They hid in the chimney corners. Next, behind the rose bushes. They hid behind the great oak trees. They hid underneath the house. They hid under the cape jessamine bushes. They hid behind the potato house. Then up in the hayloft out in the barn. They hid in the shadows of the hams hanging in the smokehouse. They hid in the thick corn and behind the pole beans out in the garden.

Now it was getting along about supper time. Uncle John came up from the fields. Cousin Omer ran to him.

"Papa! Please let us pitch dollars. Couldn't you let us have a silver dollar apiece? Couldn't you, Papa?"

Uncle John went inside the house to his secretary and drew out a long cloth bag. He counted out six silver dollars: one for each of his four youngest children and one for Eunice and Boland. "Here. Since you younger ones have to wait and eat at the second table, you can pitch while your elders eat. But, remember, I want my six dollars back."

Oh, my, who but Uncle John would give them real silver dollars to pitch? Eunice and Bo had always had to use pieces of an old broken plate. Waiting around for the older ones to eat a meal was usually an eternity, but this time it would not be a bit hard.

Out in the backyard Cousin Omer dug a round hole in the ground only slightly larger than a dollar. That was the goal. He smoothed off the surrounding hard dirt until it was slick. Twenty feet away he dug a similar hole to use as a mark to stand behind. Then he and Jesse chose sides. Eunice was on Cousin Jesse's side.

Cousin Omer was the first to get a dollar in the hole. Eunice thought of that pepper he had rubbed on her face and longed to kill his dollar by pitching hers in on top of his.

He sneered, "Coot! Coot! *You'll* never get *near* the hole." Mean old boy.

Eunice pitched. Her dollar fell a long way from the hole. On the next round Cousin Jesse's dollar landed in the hole. But nobody else's. The score was now even. Oh, if she could just show that Omer! Then Omer rang the hole again. But nobody on Jesse's team made it that round.

Omer scored again. It was three to one. Eunice's throat ached with resentment. She would get her dollar in. She would. She would. She lunged and pitched. Her dollar landed just one inch from the hole.

"Good try, Eunice!," praised Jesse.

"Oh! And so near!," sighed Lily, sympathetically.

Again both teams pitched. Eunice held her breath and hoped with all her heart as each member of her team tried. When her turn came she was determined. She toed the starting hole and swung her arm in a circle; the dollar rolled on its edge straight toward the hole, but a foot from the goal it suddenly flopped.

"Ohhhhhhhhhhh," groaned everybody on Jesse's team.

The score was still three to one when Aunt Lyddie came to the porch. "Come on, children, your turn to eat now."

As they handed their dollars back to Uncle John he spoke consolingly, "Don't any of you feel bad if you didn't land one. It's a hard game even for menfolks." Omer shouldn't have put the holes so far apart for you young ones."

But Eunice did feel bad. As the children settled themselves on the benches by the supper table, she kept thinking, "That was my chance to show Omer. And two times I came so near the hole. Only an inch away once! I'm really almost as good a pitcher as Omer and Jesse but I didn't make a single score.

Didn't score any more than if I had missed the hole by three yards."

But although Eunice was too glum to join in the talk at the table she gradually became aware of the delicious blackberry cobbler and, even better, the buttermilk. Everybody always said Aunt Lyddie made the best buttermilk in Clarke County. Eunice finished hers fast and asked, "Aunt Lyddie, could I have another glass?" It was hard to finish the second one though. Buttermilk is filling.

After supper Bo and the boys played chasing, but Cousin Lily wanted to play dolls. Eunice joined her and settled down on the floor of the gallery at Grandpa's feet.

Grandpa soon dozed. He was still very weary from the ride over from Campbell where he now lived with Brother Nap. But Eunice somehow never could lose a sense of awareness of Grandpa Griffin even though he slept. She always felt she was in the presence of somebody special—special like a book.

When Grandpa was only two years old, there had been an uprising of the Creek Indians around here. All the families had to flee to the fort with their children and belongings. But the Creeks still managed to kill Grandpa's papa, David Griffin, and his brother, Jesse; they were members of a scouting party that was ambushed by warriors. Months later reinforcements subdued the Indians, and Grandpa's Mama started home from the fort. She was on a flat boat with other women and children and their possessions. When the boat came to treacherous shoals, the women and children were put ashore to lighten the load. But the boat was wrecked just the same. Two oarsmen were drowned, and all the household goods went down. So there stood Great-Grandma Griffin and her five little children out in the woods. Her husband had been killed, and all her worldly goods were now gone. She wandered until she found kind folks who helped her reach her abandoned farm. There she had to start life all over again alone and with nothing.

Lily knew the story, too. She suggested, "Let's play Grandpa's Papa and Mama fightin' the Indians and all. The dolls can be the children."

"All right. Let's. Let's you and me be the scouting party leaving the fort."

Lily and Eunice did not openly walk down the steps. They lay flat behind the shelf of pot plants bordering the gallery and lurked behind the posts. In their eyes all the boys were Creeks.

Lily whispered, "I'm David Griffin and you're Jesse, the brother. He's the one our Jesse's named for. Remember, Eunice, if a one of those Indians sees you, you're good as dead."

They swiftly hopped down from the gallery and crawled up under the shelter of a fig tree. No harm in eating a few ripe ones if you kept your eyes open. Next they thought they'd try to make it to a crepe myrtle bush. But just as Eunice stuck her head out to see if there was danger, Cousin Jesse spied her.

"Look! Eunice's in that fig tree. MAMA. MAMA. Eunice is eating the figs you wanted to save for preserves!"

Eunice crashed to the ground. In her mind her horse rode on leaving her body behind, never to be found. That's the way it had been with Great-Grandpa Griffin when the Indians had suddenly appeared and killed him.

While they were lying dead Lily mused, "Now why don't we play the Indians have quit fighting and we're Great-Grandma on her way home on the flat boat."

Eunice and Lily ran back up the steps and hopped into a big rocker next to Grandpa's. The rocker was the flat boat. A broom was the oar. Lily was Captain.

"Stop the boat!," she commanded. "We're a-coming to the dangerous shoals. I want all the women and children put ashore to lighten the load. They can walk while we get the boat over those rocks."

Eunice obediently jumped off on to dry land.

Lily struggled with the broom. She rowed with all her might. Back and forth. Back and forth.

The plunging rocker woke Grandpa. He protested weakly, "Hon, you'd better not rock so hard. You'll turn over."

Lily ignored him. Grandpa didn't understand how hard you have to row to get over shoals. WHAM. The rocker fell over backwards.

Eunice wrung her hands. "The boat's sinking. The boat's sinking. There goes my bedstead. There goes my table and there go my candle molds! Oh, and all my quilts! Now! There go two of the men—they're drowning! Drowning! Oh, poor, poor men. Drowned. And look at us ladies and all these children. Here we are out here in the dark woods. We'll starve. Wolves and bears will eat us up."

Aunt Lyddie came to the door. "Such an imagination, Eunice. Well, time for you children to leave those wolves and bears and be going to bed. Stop your playing and come on in, all of you."

The boys made down a bed in the boys' shed room and the girls made down one in the girls' shed room. Lily and Eunice were the youngest and had to sleep on the mattress on the floor. "Cooler down here."

"Yes, and cooler without the feather bed, too."

Eunice liked the firm mattress on the floor. She loved sleeping with Sister Mattie at home, but since she only weighed about half as much as Mattie she always slept on a downhill slant. The older girls in the three big poster beds were chattering and laughing. Fresh dewy smells from outside began to slip into the house.

Lily promptly fell asleep. But not Eunice. Somehow her stomach didn't feel so good. It was beginning to seem like a tight knot. Uh, oh. Those pink-streaked peaches. She lay first on one side, then on the other, drawing up her knees. She must not wake Lily and she couldn't bring herself to tell the big girls. Aunt Lyddie and Uncle John were in bed now, too. Well, she would just have to stand it. She lay there hating herself. Nobody else had been foolish enough to eat any peaches. Why had she? Gradually the big girls all fell asleep, and there was no sound except the din the frogs were making down in the swamp. The cape jessamine odor grew heavy. Ugh. It just made her stomach feel worse. She was tossing when the clock struck eight and still tossing when it struck eight-thirty.

The knot grew almost unbearable. She perspired and clinched her fists. Oh, but it was twice as bad to be sick away from home. The clock struck nine.

Then suddenly the knot seemed to begin to untie itself. Eunice felt very grateful. Oh, what a relief. She promised herself that she would never, never again eat peaches until they were good ripe. Then she slowly groped into a blessed sleep.

When they waked in the morning the girls swiftly replaced the mattresses and began tidying the beds they had made down. Then they raced to restore order all over the house before breakfast, but when Eunice began pulling the sheets tight on Aunt Lyddie's bed, Lily stopped her. There was genuine alarm in her eyes.

"No! No! Don't touch it, Eunice!"

"Why, Lily? What's the matter?"

"Mama won't sleep in a bed made by somebody else. Never. Never. Leave it for her to make for herself."

Eunice was dumfounded. Wide-eyed she drew back from Aunt Lyddie's bed. Aunt Lyddie was so pleasant. Hard to believe she had such a strange idea. She just stood there, paralyzed, looking at it. Then they heard the breakfast bell.

Breakfast was twice as good at Uncle John's. Aunt Lyddie could make the best biscuits in the world. Grandpa Griffin thought so, too. "Lyddie, I'm losing my sight, but not my taste. Pass me another one of those biscuits, please ma'am."

Eunice ate seven and Bo ate nine.

Mama had given them strict orders to come right on home after breakfast. Eunice prodded. "Now, Bo, I went after Old Cap and put the bridle on him yesterday. Your turn this morning."

"Not me."

"Bo! You have to start taking turns. I always do everything."

Bo ignored her. Eunice knew Mama was expecting them by now and resignedly went for Old Cap. She did hate to say goodbye to Uncle John, Aunt Lyddie, Lily, and Grandpa Griffin. Not Omer, though. Yah.

When they reached home, Bo hopped down and left her to put the mule in the lot. She wished she could have left Bo at Uncle John's and brought home Cousin Lily instead. Lily always pitched in and did her share.

Coming back from the lot she suddenly thought of Sister Mattie and began to hasten. She wished she could have brought her a few of those biscuits. Mattie was looking for her, too. She was standing in the door of their room calling, "Run here, Eunice. Run."

As she ran through the back yard Eunice noticed a feather floating. Then another. And another. Why, there were feathers everywhere.

"Look!," Mattie wailed. "Look!"

The shed room was grey with feathers. Feathers on the floor. Feathers on the trunks. Feathers on the beds and on the washstand. Feathers all over the shelf where her dolls sat. But Mama and Papa's room was even worse. The chairs, the big secretary, the washstand, the sewing machine, the dresser—the entire room shrouded with feathers.

"Major did it. See? They're out of Mama and Papa's bed pillows. I was making their bed, and Mama sent for me to come to the kitchen. I left the pillows on that rocker. When I got back here, there was that little puppy ripping those pillows to bits. Oh, Eunice, please help. Let's see if we can't collect them in these pillow cases."

Eunice and Mattie swept and picked up and chased, but the more they stirred up the feathers, the faster they flew.

"I hate summer," declared Sister Mattie. "Just plain hate it. With all the doors and windows wide open this house gets so full of animals that sometimes I think there are more dogs and cats and chickens and goats inside than outside!"

 *five*

The Preachers

Monday

"Hooray! No preaching today. I've had enough to do me for awhile," yawned Sister Nora as she waked.

From the bed on the opposite side of the room Eunice caroled, "And now I can go barefooted and not dress up!"

She felt free at last. It was the Monday of the third week in August, and it would be the first day that month she wouldn't have to put on her best dress, starched pinafore, sailor hat with ribbon streamers, black stockings, and slippers and spend a long, hot day at church. The first week there had been a protracted meeting at Elam Church, a mile away. But because Elam was a Baptist Church and the Griffins were really Methodists, they also had attended protracted meeting every day the second week at the Bashi Methodist Church, three miles away.

Mama rejoiced as she put on the grits for breakfast, "Isn't it wonderful not to be up at 4 o'clock filling those trunks with food to take to the meeting?"

Sister Nora was dipping up some peach preserves out of the churn over against the wall of the dining room. "And not to be doing all that washing and ironing to keep our Sunday clothes ready again every day?"

After the necessary morning chores the whole farm slowed

down to a lazy, carefree quiet. It was the deep kind of quiet the August heat ruled.

But this respite was short lived.

A few hours later Aunt Lyddie drove by, calling from her buggy, "Look out, Lou! Look out!" She didn't even stop. The dust rose behind her and blotted out her fading image.

Mama frowned. "What on earth does Lyddie mean?"

She soon found out. When Papa cantered up on Midnight, he came right in to tell them.

"Now that the protracted meetings are over, the preachers have scheduled their Liberty Baptist Association meeting at Elam Church for the first part of this week. Since we live so close by, I felt obliged to ask some of them to stay with us. I want them to have the best we have to offer, and I want you children to behave yourselves while they are here."

Mama asked, "How many will we take, Mr. Griffin?"

"They put us down for seven."

Seven preachers. Mama didn't say a word, but her eyes grew wide, and she made the whole family june around to help her get ready.

It was, "Run, Eunice, and pick some corn. Get about five dozen ears."

"Run, Eunice, get the broom and sweep off all the galleries and walks."

" Run, Eunice, feed the chickens."

"Run to the well for more water, Eunice. And get the lye."

Lye kept the floor boards white. The floors were made of the heart of the pine; the boards were more than a foot wide. The girls scrubbed with all their might. They scrubbed the sitting room floor so hard that they raised splinters here and there. Mattie warned, "Be careful, or you'll get splinters in your bare feet and in your hands, too, Eunice."

The whole house smelled scrubbed, and the table was laden with food when the preachers arrived for supper. Eunice and

Bo came to the table. They were meek tonight. One of the preachers was invited to ask the blessing, and, my, but it was long. Eunice only half closed her eyes. She kept taking peeps at Preacher Findlay. All men wore beards, but this was by far the most impressive she had ever seen. It was thick, and it was wide, and it was long. It fell all the way to his waist. Eunice could not help thinking, "If he left off his shirt, nobody would know the difference."

Moreover, the beard was russet and it shone. It shone as if it had been brushed lovingly day after day the way Papa and Brother Ellis brushed Midnight.

When the blessing was finally over, Bo gave a great sigh of relief, but it was not so noticeable since the other six preachers and Papa were chorusing a loud "Amen." Eunice and Bo did not look at their food until they had watched Preacher Findlay carefully lay his napkin over the end of his beard. They stared as much as they dared all during the meal. Eunice wondered if some of the Old Testament prophets such as Amos or Jeremiah looked like that.

After supper Papa led the visitors out to sit on the front gallery. When the others were all settled in rockers, Papa sat down in a straight chair and propped it back against the wall. Preacher Martin lit a corncob pipe, and two others cut off a chew of tobacco.

The remaining four stirred restlessly. Then Preacher Findlay came right out and challenged the three using tobacco. "Brethren! How can we lead our flocks in the paths of righteousness if we ourselves do not set the example? Tobacco! An abomination in the sight of the Lord, and well dost thee know it."

Preacher Tyson backed him. "What availeth it for me to plead with my congregation to abandon this wickedness when they can see ministers of the gospel indulging?"

But Preacher Martin did not change the pace of his rocker.

He blew smoke and said calmly, "I for one cannot see that there is any moral question involved. Where in the scriptures are we told that there is anything wrong with a puff on a pipe?"

At this Preacher Findlay took on a zealous glow. He had preached against tobacco so often that he did not have to search for words. They flowed. His sermon could be heard all over the farm.

Out in the kitchen Sister Nora giggled. "I bet the reason *he* doesn't use tobacco is because he's so proud of that beard. Afraid he'll stain it."

Sister Mattie and Sister Mary giggled with her until Mattie came to her senses and said, "We'd better hush. They might hear us."

At this time Eunice was out back busily watering Nannygoat. She did not have to worry about feeding her: Nanny invited herself to share with nearly every other animal on the place. She was greedy, but Eunice was fond of her because she was a special present from Grandpa Holland.

Bo was dawdling happily in the backyard. After two weeks of shoes and stockings, buttoned-on pants, and a straw hat, it was wonderful to be a shirttail boy again. Like all younger boys his standard summer clothing at home was a colored homemade shirt which reached well below his knees. It was split up the sides to allow for action. He wore nothing else. No shirttail boy did.

Here came Mama from the pasture shooing the goose, the gander, and their goslings ahead of her. She had dashed down after supper to bring them up so that no varmint would harm the goslings during the night. "Run here, Eunice! Boland! I must go back inside. I'm counting on you to feed them."

Eunice and Bo ran into the garden and cropped the under leaves off the collards. This was a task they liked. Feeding the other animals was work, but feeding the goslings was a game. They threw the big green leaves down before them. The goslings ate until their bodies were full and then they kept on eating. The collards could be seen at the base of their necks. At this stage Bo exulted. "Feed 'em 'til it comes out of their mouths!" Goslings have so little down on their necks that they could look at the tube on the side of the neck and actually see the collards rising. When every neck was fully distended Bo pronounced, "They full."

Then he looked around for further amusement. There lay a stick. He picked it up and poked it at a gosling. The gander stuck out his head and snapped at him. Bo kept poking.

"Honk, honk," protested the goose. This was fun. Bo managed to get his stick under three goslings at once.

The gander hissed a warning.

Eunice turned around to watch. This gander was unusually large and vicious. Why, she couldn't count the times they had been told to stay away from him. She exclaimed, "Bo!"

But Bo poked again. The exasperated gander stretched his long neck and clamped down on Bo's shirt-tail. "Let go of me," yelled Bo.

The gander held on. Bo hopped like a frog. The great gander held on. Bo tried to reach the gander with the stick. The gander evaded him with no trouble. Bo tried running around and around in circles. The gander sometimes all but sailed through the air, but he held on.

"You let go of me! You let go of me!" But the gander was big and strong. He was going to teach this little boy well.

Bo ran up the steps to the kitchen. He dashed across the porch and around the raised wooden walk to the house. The gander still held on. They ran right through the shed room and sitting room.

On the front gallery Preacher Findlay was pointing his finger at Preacher Martin and thundering, "And I say unto you, 't was sin that caused the downfall of Babylon. Sin that caused the downfall of Jerusalem. Sin that ended the glory that was Rome . . ."

Out from the sitting room burst Bo. You could see his whole naked body because the gander had his back shirt-tail pulled out and up. Bo wept, "Get me loose! Get me loose! He won't let go!"

Up sprang Papa and the preachers. They surrounded the two. Some pulled Bo and some pulled the gander. It was a real tug of war.

Sister Nora called out, "Wait! I'll get the scissors and cut the shirt-tail!"

Off she ran to look for the scissors. The gander might have held on forever if he had not become so annoyed with the men that he was tempted to snap at them. Preacher Findlay took hold of the gander's neck. His sweeping russet beard rippled down and the angry gander forsook Bo to turn and snap at it instead. Bo crashed forward on his knees.

Now the gander had the glorious beard in his mouth and glared straight into Preacher Findlay's eyes. Both were furious.

Sister Nora came running back with the scissors. With a mock heroic air she unhesitatingly whacked off the part of the beard the gander held. Part of the beard—no. Almost all. Now it was cut more than halfway across and almost up to his chin.

Poor Mr. Findlay. He would have been ashamed to admit how vain he was about his flowing beard. It was the last thing he would have ever sacrificed. And this merely to release a little boy from a gander. He felt robbed of his very identity. And naked. Downright naked. Why, that Nora Griffin was a Delilah. That's what she was.

"A fine how-de-do," said Mama as she marched Boland off to bed. "A fine how-de-do. Mercy day. Boland, are you *sure* you didn't do something to provoke that gander? You must have. You have no foresight about you, child. Not a bit. You never stop and think before you start something."

The irate gander spat out the beard contemptuously. Then he walked haughtily around the cape jessamine bushes and returned to his family.

Sister Nora reappeared with some old copies of the *Atlanta Journal* and spread them on the floor of the gallery. She set a chair on them and beckoned. "Here, Brother Findlay. Do sit here and let me shape up your beard a little. I've really made a mess of it, haven't I?"

She didn't dare look in Papa's direction.

❀ six

The Preachers' Return

Tuesday

The next morning at dawn the women and girls were all up preparing thick slices of ham, sausage patties, fresh eggs, grits, hot biscuits, fritters, preserves, jelly, and coffee for breakfast.
    The preachers ate round after round after round. The sausage platter was empty. The fritter platter was empty. There was not another drop of coffee. Then Preacher Tyson took the very last biscuit, saying, "Well, now, I don't mind if I do." Mama decided they'd better start cooking again, but just then the men began to place their forks and pearl-handled knives across their plates and put their napkins on the table. It was a relief to hear them rise and push back the benches. Some saddled their horses, and some hitched up their buggies, and they all rode away to spend the day at church.
    As soon as he was sure they had all left, Papa came into the dining room where Eunice was sweeping the crumbs off the sandy floor. "Eunice, is your mother back here?"
    Mama appeared at the door of the stove room.
    Papa said to her, "I would think, Miss Lou, that you would also have offered the brethren some fried chicken and rice and gravy for their breakfast. I was embarrassed."
    Mama replied sincerely and graciously, "I am sorry, Mr.

Griffin. There'll be chicken for breakfast the rest of their stay. I don't know what was the matter with me."

Sister Nora flounced in as soon as Papa left. "Why do they have to be fed like kings? Why wouldn't sausage and ham and eggs and fritters and biscuits do for anybody? Mama! I put out three kinds of preserves and four kinds of jelly!"

Mama defended Papa. "Now, Nora. The preachers are paid so little that none of them could live unless they were farmers, too. Papa thinks that we can at least show our appreciation by honoring them with the best that we have."

Nora cooled down. "Yes ma'am. But I know one thing. *I'll* never marry one. They eat forever and they talk forever."

Again that day Mama made all the wage-hands and children june around every minute. She was determined to please Papa. Not even Boland was allowed to play.

Wednesday

Wednesday morning at four o'clock Mama and Sister Mattie went out to the hen house with a determined air. And by the time the sun came up, there was a great platter of fried chicken on the dining room table. The rest of the breakfast was equally magnificent, and Papa did not need to feel apologetic in any wise.

After breakfast Eunice went out to the washhouse and helped Sister Mattie scrub out all the cedar buckets. This was a regular Wednesday chore and a hard one. After they scoured the insides of the buckets, they also had to polish the brass bands around the outside with corncobs dipped in wood ashes. The buckets had to be kept spotless because they held all the drinking water. At all times there was a row of them on a shelf on the shady end of the front gallery together with the dipper, basin, and towel.

As the girls worked, Cephas was sicking Nannygoat onto Felix. "Butt him, Nanny! Go on. Butt that boy. A goat who can't butt ain't no goat."

Eunice said, "You hear that, Mattie? You see them? It really is hard for me to train my Nannygoat to act right when the boys are all so busy teaching her to chase people and butt 'em."

Sister Mattie looked uncertain. "I know. But that's not as bad as the way she eats her way right through the house. The idea of walking right into Mama's room and eating that beautiful paper screen we had in front of the fireplace. Poor Sister Maggie worked months to make that and was so proud of it. As much as I love you, Eunice, I can't defend your goat! Why, I wouldn't be surprised if she follows us to church and eats her way down the aisle at my wedding."

Eunice signed. Mattie was still planning to marry Mr. Kimbrough. Eunice could not even bear to think of it. She would have no ally when Mattie left. Sister Mary and Sister Nora were inseparable. There was no possibility among those teasing brothers. Mama was understanding and kind like Mattie, but after all, she was in the position of Mama. No, there could be no replacement for Mattie.

Sister Mattie began splashing clear water on her face and pouring a little across her wrists. "Oh, but this is a hot day. If it's this bad before eight o'clock in the morning, think what it will be later on. And all the preachers still here."

By supper time the heat was sickening.

Mama said, "It's so sultry that there are even more flies than usual tonight. All three of you older girls had better stand and fan them away while the preachers eat."

Sister Mary and Sister Nora scrambled for the paper fans. There were only two, and they didn't want to be the ones who had to go out and get a branch off the mulberry tree. They had made the fans by attaching strips of crepe paper to a long cane. Mary and Nora were class conscious when it came to fans. They envied Brother Nap's wife, Sister Arco, who had one suspended from the ceiling, which she could pull by a cord as she sat at the foot of the table. Even so they were a little bit proud of their own since they had used crepe paper, and they knew some families who could afford only newspaper.

Mary stood at the head of the table with the pink fan. It matched her pink dotted swiss dress. Nora was in the center with the blue fan. It matched her beautiful eyes. Mattie was too grown-up to be ashamed of her mulberry branch. She was in charge of the foot of the table, which was by the door.

In trooped the preachers and the remainder of the family. Preacher Nichols returned thanks. Preacher Nichols paused often. It was very difficult to feel reverent during the awkward silences. Eunice felt perspiration trickling down her legs.

Preacher Nichols had not even finished thanks when Major, the puppy, came tripping in the door. Sister Mattie thought it might save confusion not to shoo him out until the prayer was over. But the next time Preacher Nichols paused, Major barked. A second time he paused, and Major barked again. The prayer was hastily ended. Sister Mattie then used her leafy branch to force Major outside.

Platter after platter of fried chicken, ham, and roast beef were passed. Slaw, rice, green peppers, string beans, okra, mustard, corn on the cob, fried corn, butter beans, boiled potatoes, black-eyed peas, chow-chow, and cucumbers went around and around.

Eunice looked up and saw her nanny goat coming in. She was accompanied by a Rhode Island Red hen. Nanny looked eagerly at all the food on the table. But Sister Mattie swooped down. She commanded in a hoarse whisper, "Get out of here and get back into that yard!"

Mama took every meat platter out to the kitchen and refilled it. She filled all the vegetable bowls time after time. They brought in self-rising bread, corn bread, and biscuits time and again. Cephas brought two more buckets of water from the well. He went back to the well for another great cooler filled with sweet milk and another filled with buttermilk.

Sister Mary pressed her handkerchief to her forehead. Her fan moved languidly.

Eunice suddenly realized that she smelled fresh coffee and heard the noise of hot fat popping out in the kitchen. Mama must have become frantic and started cooking again! Sure enough, in a few minutes Mama brought in a platter of fried steak, and shortly afterwards Sister Mattie went out and came in with another. At the very sight Sister Nora went over and leaned far out of the window for air.

Eunice was sure there was never such interminable talking and eating and never such a hot night. She wished she could reach over and pick up the carving knife and whack off both her pigtails.

A full two hours and a half passed before their plates were taken away, and the Jeff Davis pie was served. By now even valiant Sister Mattie could no longer conceal her weariness. She was as drooped as the leaves on her mulberry branch. At last the company finished the pie, and rose. "Mrs. Griffin, I never tasted better Jeff Davis pie," chorused several of the men as they left the dining room.

Eunice slipped around to her sisters who were still fanning flies. "Here, I'll fan while y'all eat. Not much left, though, is there?"

As the girls sank down at the table Brother Ellis came clattering up the steps. "Eunice! Your Nannygoat has eaten up Preacher Tyson's Testament. He left it on the table in the company room, and Nanny walked right in and ate it while we were at supper. It was Mr. Tyson's new gold-edged Testament with a red ribbon marker! You should just see the mess she made."

Papa was outdone. This was more than he could bear. He had wanted his guests honored, and instead they had suffered indignity. First, Boland and the gander and the beard cutting. Then, no fried chicken for breakfast. Now Nanny's mischief was too much.

He strode in. "Ootchie, you heard. You'll just have to sell that goat and use the money to replace Preacher Tyson's Testament. It's not your fault that she's such a nuisance, but we can't put up with her any longer. She's just too destructive to keep."

Eunice held in until Papa was gone. Then she wept.

"It's not fair. Nanny's not any worse than Major! Major tears up just as much. And it was Bo who poked at the goslings—not me! I didn't do a single thing, and here I'm the one who has to sell my nanny goat. I'm going to tell Grandpa Holland. He gave me Nanny for my very own, and he won't like it either. It's not fair. Not fair. Not fair."

❊ seven

The Ugly Stage

Day's store sold those big fat bunches of stick candy for a nickel. The last Saturday in September Bo and Eunice fell to discussing that candy and wanting some so much that they could hardly bear it. "Mama, couldn't you let us have a dozen eggs to trade for some candy?"

"That's foolishness, and you two know it. But, all right. I'll give in this one time. If you'll gather the eggs, you can take them over when you go for the mail this evening."

That evening as they padded over to the store in the dust, Eunice began thinking aloud. "As bad as I want that candy I wonder if sardines wouldn't be even better. A whole great big can full! And all the crackers both of us could eat—think of that, Bo."

"I'm thinkin' of that. I want sardines, too. But I still vote for candy this time."

"Wouldn't it be wonderful if they'd allow us a dime for the eggs instead of just a nickel?"

"Then we could have both!"

Before they reached the store they caught up with their nearest neighbor, Mr. Walker. He gave them his customary greeting in his high, high, voice. "Uh huh. Hey-o, Eunice. Hey-o, Boland."

Together they clattered up the wooden steps of the long country store. It was crowded today. There was Mr. Jarvis,

Papa's horse-loving friend who had gone with him to Mobile and chosen Midnight. Mrs. Williams, Newell's Mama. Mr. Walker's sister, Miss Mandy, picking out a calico. Several of Mr. Dave White's big boys from over at St. David. The center of attention was Miss Nin Hill. She had a baby squirrel, which she had tamed. She had named it Lucy. At the moment Lucy was eating from Bryant White's hand.

Eunice and Bo were entranced. "Oh, Miss Nin, how did you tame her? Squirrels just run from us."

"Lucy won't. Here." She placed Lucy on Eunice's shoulder. Lucy stayed there contentedly and allowed Eunice to stroke her.

"Well, we must be on our way now, Lucy," said Miss Nin. Lucy obediently ran down Eunice and trotted out the door and down the steps behind her mistress.

"Oh, my, look at that," Eunice sighed enviously.

Bo stayed up in the front of the store to swap the eggs, and Eunice went to the post-office section in the back to ask for the mail. There was sure to be the *Clarke County Democrat* and the *Atlanta Journal* if nothing more.

The postmaster was Miss Nin's brother, Mr. Os Hill. Mr. Os wore a little scoop of an eyeshade. His moustache curled up at the sides in a grand manner. He looked out over his tremendous paunch with a superior air because he was the former school teacher. He had taught everybody's grown brothers and sisters and parents and still treated them all like children.

Mr. Os looked down at Eunice as he handed her the mail and announced crisply, "Yunnis, you're in the ugly stage."

He shook his head at her as if she were hopeless and repeated, "The ugly stage."

For a moment she was frozen in humiliation. Everybody in the store had heard him. Mr. Jarvis, Mrs. Williams, Mr. Walker, Miss Mandy, the White boys, the clerks, Carl and Tom Day. Everybody had heard and now stood still, listening.

Then she somehow managed to breathe enough to move and went over to nudge Bo. "Come on."

As they hastened out through the pepper and cheese and new-shoes smell of the store it seemed five times as long as it ever had before. If Bo hadn't already swapped the eggs for the candy, she wouldn't have stayed to do it. She was all choked up. Her throat was so dry it ached. It was a relief to get down the steps and on the road home.

"I hate old man Os. He's mean, mean, mean. Thinks he knows it all. If he knows so much, why can't he even learn to say my name right. Always calls me *Yunnis*. Mama says Eunice was the mother of Timothy in the Bible and that anybody ought to be able to say *You-niss*."

Then she wheeled around and looked at Bo accusingly. "You—well, why aren't you in the ugly stage if I am? You haven't got a single front tooth. Look at that big round belly. Oh, you're a boy, and it doesn't matter how you look. But me. I'm just a miserable in-between girl. Not a baby to coo over. Not a grown up girl with her hair in a ball. Just nothing."

She relieved her anger by crunching her share of the candy canes to pieces instead of sucking them slowly.

When they reached home, Bo told it. "SiBattie, Mr. Os Hill says Eunice is in the ugly stage. He said it right out loud in the store."

"Oh, how silly," said Sister Mattie with an air of dismissal. "Don't pay any attention to him. All children look spindly when they suddenly grow several inches taller, and Eunice's new teeth are large for her face now because they're the ones she'll have when she's grown. Everybody grows in some places faster than in others. What does it matter? Don't you worry a bit, Eunice."

The next afternoon when Sunday School was over Eunice ran to the girls' shed room to get out of her good clothes. Her older sisters were all but ripping off their best dresses. October had come today, but the heat had not yet lessened.

Sister Mattie stepped out of her second petticoat. "A crowd of us are going over to The Big Gully to hunt berries and nuts. If you'll hurry, Eunice, and get ready, you can come, too."

As the girls emerged from their shed room, Mama glanced up and was horrified. "Girls! Your bonnets! No one but Nora has on a bonnet! Mama was not going to let a daughter of hers get freckled and brown.

Mattie put on her blue checked gingham bonnet, and Mary wore a white ruffled one. Eunice put on her new sun hat. She had made it by cutting all the cabbage roses off the brim of Sister Mattie's discarded yellow straw hat. But it did not stay on very well. The tiny crown just would not pull down far enough on her head. Eunice asked, "Mama, may I borrow your scissors?"

She cut the offending crown out of the hat. Now the hole was big enough so that the brim would pull down around her head far enough. It felt firm. The brim was narrow in back and on the sides, but it was more than a foot wide in front.

Mama approved. "Now. That ought to protect you."

All the young folks carried ten-pound lard buckets to the Big Gully, but Eunice wouldn't take one. "I'll put mine in your buckets," she offered. Eunice was not being generous. She just wanted to be free to jump gullies and ride little pine trees without having to hang onto something.

The Big Gully was nearer the Days' than home. It was a red clay canyon, deeper than a two-story house is high. It was the best place of all for finding berries and nuts.

First they came to a big sloe tree. The young folks began shaking the lower limbs and tapping the top ones with poles to make the sloes fall. Eunice didn't stop, though. Sloes made good jelly and jam, but they were too sour to eat. She wanted to help gather something you could sample. She went on ahead and found a persimmon tree to climb. She picked two and sat in a crotch in the tree to eat them. But one she decided not to eat after all. It wasn't quite ripe. She didn't want to get her mouth all drawn up and puckered.

Mr. Kimbrough came over to join her. "Eunice, aren't you going to take some to your mother for pies?"

"Oh, no, sir. Mama never makes persimmon pie. She just lets us eat ours. Here, you take some of these." She hopped down and looked around. Here and there were fall huckleberries, which were ripening. Mama didn't make pies out of fall huckleberries either, so all the Griffins had a good excuse for eating those, too.

But they restrained themselves when they found vines full of possum grapes, because Mama did like to pack those down in a stone crock with layers of sugar to make grape wine and to dip out some occasionally to make winey-tasting plate pies.

There were chinquapin trees in the gully, too, but Eunice would not touch them. Too horny. She could never get enough chinquapins to eat, but even so she avoided the trees. She stood back and watched gratefully as some big boys knocked down the nuts with poles. Then she picked them up diligently. She did hope they'd take home a lot of them.

Someone called, "Scaly barks over here!"

But Eunice stayed with the chinquapins. Scaly barks were too hard to crack. She held her skirt out in front of her and filled it full. Holding it carefully she walked cautiously to Brother Fowler's bucket. She let the nuts funnel down the fold of her dress into the bucket and straightened up.

Meanwhile, somebody had come near. She looked up to see who it might be. There stood Mr. Os Hill, the postmaster. He had heard all the noise and come over to join in. Oh, my! She was still smarting from his ill treatment yesterday. It didn't seem fair to have to face him again so soon. Her worst fears were soon realized.

Mr. Os looked at Eunice, threw back his head, and laughed like a goat. "Yunnis, is that a hat?"

He laughed his goat laugh so hard that everybody else began to chuckle. The boys thought it was funny. They joined in, "Yunnis, is that a hat?"

Such a din. The very hills began to echo, "Yunnis, is that a hat?"

Yesterday and now today. It was bad enough to have the kid boys picking on her. But here Mr. Os was, grown up, and the meanest one of them all.

Off and on all the way home the boys would chant, "Yunnis, is that a hat?"

She would have thrown it into the bushes and abandoned it if she had not known that it would make Mama unhappy to have her yield to her bad temper as well as be out in the sun bareheaded. Mama, if no one else, had thought it a fine sun hat.

When the house was in sight Eunice scampered ahead of the young folks. She raced to the shade of the porch and yanked off the hat. Mr. Os and those big boys. She despised them all.

❀ eight
The Wedding

Sister Mattie's wedding to Mr. Marion Kimbrough was going to be stylish. So stylish, in fact, that Sister Arco came over from Campbell to supervise the preparations for the infare after the ceremony. She was the wife of Bud Nap, Eunice's oldest brother, and an expert at fancy cookery.

The very last day before the wedding every person on the farm worked feverishly. While the preparations for the feast were going on out back, Mama was frantically helping Sister Mattie and Grandma Holland with the last minute details of the wedding dress and trousseau. As she measured a hem, Mama took a pin out of her mouth long enough to call to Eunice, "Run, Eunice! Get your shoes shined and all your Sunday clothes clean and ironed and ready. Look over Boland's clothes, too, and make him shine his shoes."

Eunice went to the smokehouse for some of the tallow they always saved when they killed a beef. She reached up into the chimney for a handful of soot. This she squeezed through and through the tallow until it blended into a soft black paste.

She fetched Boland's shoes. Easier to polish them herself than to plead with Bo. Then picked up her own good slippers. Her heart sank. There in the toe of the right slipper was a hole. A hole all the way through. She must have been too tired to notice when she last took them off. "Mama! Mama! There's a hole in my shoe. I *can't* wear it to the wedding. I have to have some new ones."

"Oh, mercy day, Eunice. That little hole? Nobody'll ever notice it on a galloping horse. Why, I'm not even sure we're going to have Mattie ready. Looks as if she's going to walk down the aisle with no wedding veil and go away in a second-day dress with the button holes not worked and the hem tagging down. Nobody has time to worry about you today, child."

"But, Mama, I can go to the store by myself."

"Eunice! Don't nag me. You know there is no money left after all this."

Eunice got a tight feeling down in her throat. She was sure everybody would notice. She hoped that tomorrow she would wake up sick, sick, sick and not even have to be seen. Maybe measles. Maybe malaria. She prayed, "Lord, give me high fever."

"Run here, Eunice!" Sister Arco had overheard, and, seeing that Eunice was upset, attempted to distract her. "Eunice, don't you want to watch me make the gelatine?

Eunice ran. She had heard Sister Arco telling Mama and the big girls about the exciting new dessert Bud Nap now sold in his store. "See, Eunice? I told you we were going to have something new and beautiful to eat. Red gelatine. And it's easy to make, too. Help me empty the packages into this big pan" Package after package of the pink grainy powder they unwrapped and emptied.

"Now, stand back, Eunice, while I pour the boiling water on it. Watch." Sister Mary, Sister Nora, Felix, and Bo gathered to watch, too. As Sister Arco poured the hot water on the pink grains they turned deep red. The bowl was now full of beautiful red liquid. She stirred it.

"I'm stirring to make sure it all dissolves. But that's all we have to do. Not another thing. We'll set it in a cool place, and it'll just congeal itself. Now, Eunice, would you and Bo and Felix like to lick the papers that were around the gelatine?"

Each immediately claimed a paper and began tasting. Even Sister Mary and Sister Nora could not resist a few licks. Sister Arco laughed, "It really doesn't give you any idea of the way the gelatine will taste tomorrow."

On the morning of Sister Mattie's wedding day Nora and Mary waked Eunice by getting up before sunrise to pick the flowers to decorate the church and the dining room.

As they stepped into their petticoats, Mary whispered, "Why don't we use just pink and white roses and octobers in the church? Seems to me it would look better than mixing in the yellow and bronze."

"A good idea. But don't you think the yellow and bronze would be all right on the table at the infare?"

"Not the bronze. Not with the red gelatine. Let's just use all white on the table. Looks more like a wedding, and so sumptuous."

Sister Nora sighed. "Oh, if only there were an organ for a little music. They tell me the Baptists in Thomasville have one now."

Sister Mary teased, "Don't worry. Even Elam will have one by the time you settle down to one sweetheart."

Sister Mattie lay there smiling at the wall and not saying a word.

Eunice wished she shared the girls' pleasure in the occasion. But she did not. Outside the weather sparkled and beckoned. Yet the day ahead confronted Eunice like a dank, sheer cliff. She looked herself over hopefully to see if she might be breaking out with anything. There was nothing. She tried vainly to summon sniffles. None. No, not one excuse to hide herself all day long.

Immediately after breakfast Nora and Mary arranged a great glass bowl of white roses and octobers to use on the table at the infare. Brother Fowler hitched up the buggy for them, and the two girls then dashed off to the church to decorate it and get home again before time to dress.

But Sister Mattie had to take her time. She reached for her pipe and the jar of Life Everlasting. She laughed as she sat in a rocker to smoke it, "I certainly don't want to wheeze at my wedding."

In order to transport the entire family to Elam Church, Papa and the boys had to hitch up the wagon as well as the buggy. Then they saddled two of the horses for two of the boys to ride. Eunice and Bo came out and climbed up onto the little bench in the back of the seat of the buggy in which Papa, Mama, and Sister Mattie were to ride. Bo always called this little bench their "hiner seat." Papa had given the buggy such a cleaning that it looked almost new. He had curried and brushed Midnight until she glistened. The brass on the harness shone.

Papa's little moustache was clipped just so, and his small sharp beard was carefully trimmed. Mama, as always, appeared in a cape, and today it was her ruffled pale gray taffeta, which Sister Arco had made for her.

Then out came Sister Mattie in her wedding dress. Eunice gasped. Here was a dress of wondrous beauty. Grandma Holland had made it. Grandma was the one the big rich folks engaged to make their wedding dresses, and she had declared, "This one is for my own granddaughter, and it's going to be the finest I have ever made."

It was of heavy ivory satin. There was no lace, no fuss, not even a waistline or belt. It was cut and draped to show the beauty of the fabric. Grandma had adapted it from a picture in a *Delineator* and sounded like the magazine when she described it. "A princess dress with draped front and bell back, having a slight train."

"A *princess* dress is right," thought Eunice.

Mattie's shoes and gloves were of the softest white kid. Small wonder that nobody else in the family could have new clothes at the same time.

As Papa helped Mattie into the buggy, she gave Eunice a smile. "Eunice, how nice that you'll be back there to hold my veil for me!"

Off they rode with Mattie's veil falling over the back of the buggy seat and Eunice holding it with great care and fierce pride. It was a long, long ride, but not once did she relax. What a sight that red clay dust could make of that long veil.

When they reached Elam Church, Bo hopped down from the hiner seat almost before Papa stopped Midnight. Not Eunice. She slid off languidly, and Papa and Mama almost had to drag her up the church steps.

Sister Mattie was to wait outside. Everybody else was already in the church and seated. If only Eunice could have stopped at the back row. But, no, the family of the bride was to sit up front alongside the pulpit in the old men's amen corner. She saw all her older brothers and sisters: Brother Nap, Sister Maggie, and Brother Horrie (Bud), as well as those still at home. Grandpa and Grandma Holland. Grandpa Griffin, too. Feeble and poorly now, but he had insisted on coming over from Campbell with Nap. None of the cousins, though. Too many. They were out in the regular pews. The only empty space left in the amen corner was in the front row. They had saved it for the parents of the bride.

Papa grasped Boland's hand and Mama took Eunice's, and down the aisle they went. Every head turned, stared at her toe, and watched every step she took. She was certain of it. She could hear them thinking, "Eunice's toe is out. Poking right up out of a hole in her shoe. And at her own sister's wedding. Disgraceful!"

The pink and white roses and octobers softened the unpainted, weathered interior of the frame church. Elam Church was like a plain woman who can ill afford to deck herself with strong colors; Mary and Nora had somehow sensed this.

Eunice looked across the pulpit. Mr. Kimbrough's family was in the old ladies' amen corner opposite them. She examined them anxiously. It would be dreadful if they were not good to Mattie. Well, she thought as she scanned each face, they look about as kind as anybody does when they're all laced up in corsets and best shoes.

Preacher Findlay came in from the side door behind her and stood in front of the pulpit. Down the aisle came Sister Mattie and Mr. Kimbrough together. The congregation turned and looked admiringly at the handsome couple. Sister Mattie. There was never a bride in the *Delineator* magazines to compare, thought Eunice loyally.

Soon Preacher Findlay was saying, "Do you, Martha Belle, take this man to be your lawful wedded husband . . .forsaking all others . . ."

Forsaking all others. Eunice heard nothing more.

She welcomed the confusion after the ceremony. She dodged in and out of the crowd, never pausing, mindful of her shoe and remembering what Mama had said about it never being noticed on a galloping horse.

She leapt up onto the hiner seat and hid her feet under the front seat as she waited for the others. As soon as they reached home, she slipped out behind the barn. Almost immediately she could hear the folks beginning to arrive for the infare. Felix happened along. To him she spoke her bitter thoughts. "How can I go to school tomorrow? They'll all be whispering and giggling. They'll all be saying, "Eunice turned up at Mattie's wedding with her toe poking up out of her shoe."

Felix comforted her. "Now, Miss Newnich, no sense in worryin'. Yo' shoe is black and yo' stocking is black. Nobody is seeing yo' toe but you. Come on, let's us go watch 'em cut that big cake."

Eunice trailed behind Felix, and from the kitchen they watched the company. The dining room was a place of splendor. No faded oil cloth on the table today. The great white damask cloth covered it, and all Mama's cut glass gleamed. In the center of the table was the large bowl of white roses and white octobers. Mary had been right about all-white looking sumptuous.

The platters of ham, turkey, spareribs, and the deep chicken pies went around and around and around. The oven door banged out batch after batch of hot biscuits. Finally, when everybody refused another helping, Mama, Aunt Lyddie, and Sister Mary cleared the table. Then Eunice and Felix had to squeeze back into a corner to make room for Sister Arco who brought out the great tiered wedding cake. Next came tray after tray of tiny tea cakes iced in colors and designs. Some had wee candies sprinkled on top.

Then Mary and Nora brought in the dishes of red gelatine, quivering and sparkling. The company gasped at the sight.

"Can't wait to taste it!," sang out Aunt Lyddie.

Mrs. Day said admiringly, "Arco is always so up-to-date." Then she turned and gave Mr. Day an accusing glance. No red gelatine in Mr. Day's store. Why did he let Nap Griffin's store over in Campbell get ahead of him?

All over the room people were murmuring, "Delicious!"

"Tastes as good as it looks!"

"Count on Arco Griffin to come up with something new and fashionable."

Eunice told Felix, "I'm not bothering with dinner today. Let's just sit on the kitchen porch steps with cakes and our gelatine." They chose the tea cakes with the most icing and candies on top, and Sister Arco topped their gelatine with whipped cream before they bore it off to the steps. Mama was too busy to notice that they had selected an all-dessert meal.

Bo came out to join them. He was blissfully stuffed. "Wish they'd all get married."

For a moment Eunice forgot to be miserable. "Hope there are some of these little cakes left over. Think of having these to take to school in our lunch buckets."

The following morning Sister Mattie put on her second-day dress of brown cashmere trimmed with heavy gold braid and prepared to leave with Mr. Kimbrough. Today his family was having another infare in their honor at Choctaw Corner. Brother Ellis, Sister Nora, and Sister Mary were going along to enjoy the party.

Mr. Kimbrough had an ordinary uncovered buggy, but he had borrowed a top-buggy for this occasion, and he drove it around to the front gate with a flourish.

Mattie was saying her good-byes. "Now, Papa, any time anybody goes to Thomasville, remind them to be sure to stop on the way to see me. Remember, it's the first two-story house with a fenced lane leading back to it. Sits way back from the road. A pear grove on each side."

She gave Eunice a long, special hug and kiss. "I'll miss you so much. You'll just have to come up for a stay with us at Choctaw Corner soon."

As they rode away Bo asked, "Who lent Mr. Kimbrough a top-buggy?"

Mama brushed away tears and choked as she corrected him. "Not Mr. Kimbrough. He's your Brother Marion now."

Eunice couldn't say a word. When the buggy was out of sight, she went out back and stirred a stick aimlessly in an empty black iron wash pot. Grandpa Griffin came slowly toward her, feeling his way with his cane. "I wouldn't go off and leave *her*," blurted out Eunice.

"Now, Eunice. Why she's nearly ten years older than you, hon. Suppose she waited until you get ready to marry, too. Why, she'd be an old woman."

❈ nine

Pastimes

It was a sparkling Saturday morning the second week of November. The merciless sun had relaxed into such friendliness that Eunice and Bo wore cloaks until after breakfast.

"Good day for slidin'."

"Yes, but Woodley mistook our slides for trash and burned them under the wash pot. We've got to make some more."

Woodley was a wage-hand. The reason he had unwittingly tossed their slides into the fire was that they were only staves from hogsheads.

"Look over there by the barn. That hogshead has a place bashed in it. Papa won't care if we get two staves off it."

Just as they succeeded in detaching two staves, Brother Bunyan passed by and volunteered help. "Here, let me just nail a cleat on the foot of these staves for you to brace your feet on. And I'll leave the middle nail standing up a bit so you can tie a rope on it to hold onto and drag it by."

The steepest hill for sliding was away over across the fields. The two of them started off toward it dragging their slides. But before they had gone very far, Bo threw down his rope and went dancing off ahead. "Here, Eunice, you bring mine for me."

Oh, that aggravating little Bo. Eunice was tempted to leave his slide behind. Instead she grimly tugged both. It was hard. The slides banged together. They foundered upon clumps of grass and clay. The ropes tangled. Eunice wondered whether any sliding could be worth all this.

But when she finally reached their chosen hill, her enthusiasm returned. It was glistening slick with a thick covering of brown pine needles varying from an inch deep in the thinnest spot to two feet deep in the drifts around the tree trunks. Virgin long-leaf pines did not grow very close together. In fact they had seen Papa drive a full-size wagon through a pine forest if he had a good enough reason.

"Look, Bo, I've caught an opening. We can slide all the way down here and not hit a thing." Eunice nestled down within the curve of the stave, braced her feet against the cleat, held the rope, clinched her teeth, held her breath, and made a slight movement with her hips which started the slide.

Down, down, down the great long sweep she raced screaming with excitement. Bo whizzed behind her. Toward the bottom she thrust her heels out into the pine needles and gradually slowed down and stopped. Perfect. She didn't know why she'd been so scared.

Then back up the great hill they tugged again. "Don't know why they don't call these hills mountains. They are sure long and steep enough."

Down, down, down again and again they slid, each trip prefixed by a toiling ascent. After seven trips down Eunice continued sitting on her stave and panted, "I'm just going to sit here and blow a minute."

Bo sat chewing a pine needle. "Eunice, do you see what I see? Just look at that muscadine vine. That one's the granddaddy of 'em all." The weathered gray vine twisted up, up, up and disappeared somewhere in the shadows among the top branches of the giant tree. "If it's up there good, it's long enough to swing from here to kingdom come. You could get out over those little trees and across the branch and clear over to the middle of that next hill."

"Whooooooo, Boland. Mama'd die if she knew."

"She ain't going to know if you don't tell her."

"She'd know if the vine broke and you got hurt."

"Well, I'm going to test it good first." Bo swung a piece o' way, and the gnarled old vine held. He swung farther out, and it held. Farther and farther each time. Now he was floating over the tops of the berry-flecked dogwood and holly trees. Now clear out over the willows alongside the branch. Now spang over the branch. Now across to the other hill.

It was a sight to see. Bo's round cheeks were always red, but now his whole face was, too. Eunice could not bear watching him have all the fun. She was ready to try it. "My turn, my turn," she shouted. Bo's hands and arms were getting tired. He let the cat die. Eunice was 4 years older but was so thin that she weighed no more than her chubby brother. "If it'll hold you, I know it'll hold me."

Off she swung with her calico skirt billowing and pigtails flying. This was practically as good as being a blue jay or a butterfly. She looked down at her clumpy old brass-toed shoes skimming right over the tops of the willows. Eunice had never felt this free. As she wafted all the way over to the other hill, she realized that she was a little contemptuous of the earth-bound creature she used to be.

The sound of the dinner horn brought her back to reality. "Make the cat die fast, Eunice. If we're too late for dinner Mama'll want to know what we've been up to."

At the dinner table Bo finished his second piece of the sugary crusted muscadine pie and leaned over to Eunice. "We going to fish today?"

That was a foolish question. They always fished on Saturday and any other day they had a little free time. Not that they ever caught any. "Oh, we might as well go. But, Bo, you have to promise to carry your share. You always expect me to carry everything."

Out they went for their poles and strings and tin can for bait. "You know, Bo, I believe we spend more time digging for bait than we do fishing."

"Maybe that's why we don't ever catch any fish."

They always fished over at Grandma and Grandpa Holland's place. Fishing was better over there. Besides, it was worth the walk to stop at the house to get some of Grandma's molasses cake. She kept a fifty-pound lard can full because Grandpa Holland liked to eat it when he rose early to work in the fields a few hours before breakfast.

"Grandma," Eunice said to her today as she reached in the can, "when I get married, don't bother to make me any tall stack of white cakes. I'd-a lot rather have this kind." Eunice and Boland wolfed down great slabs of the moist cake.

Grandma whipped out a big pan and began filling it with skinned rabbits. "Mr. Holland killed five rabbits this morning, and we'll never eat them all. You children take some home with you. And, wait. Don't leave yet. I'm going to the house and get a ball of red yarn I promised your Mama. You can just take the things along with you and remember to take them home when you're through fishing. But be sure to keep the rabbits in the shade."

Down the hill to the little stream they hurried. This turned out to be a good day. They caught five tiny fishes.

When it was time to start home, Eunice tried in vain to start up the hill with the poles, the bait can, the string of fish, the pan of rabbits, and the yarn. "Which will you carry, Boland?"

"Carry nuthin'! I'm chunkin' birds."

"Boland Griffin, you don't play fair. Not once have you

ever carried anything. I'm not supposed to wait on you forever. Now I'm just leaving the fish and the bait can on this stump, and they're going to stay there until you bring 'em. The poles and rabbits and yarn are the messy things and more than my share."

When they came trailing through the orchard Papa called out gaily, "Been fishin'?"
"Yes, sir."
"Over at The Whip's?" The Whip was Papa's name for Grandma. They could never fathom why. Whenever they asked him he would just grin.
"Yes, sir."
"How many'd you catch?"
"Five."
"Five! Where are they?"
"On a stump," Eunice shouted defiantly. "I left 'em back on a stump with the bait can. Going to stay there, too, until that lazy Bo brings them."
"Ootchie. What's gotten into you? You know better than that! You don't leave fish on a stump. Either leave them in the creek to live or bring them home to eat. The idea of taking those fish out of water and leaving them there to die and just be wasted. You're old enough to know better than that, Eunice."
Papa reached up for a switch off a peach tree. He was just thinking how ridiculous it was to abandon the fish. He did not realize that for days and weeks and months and years Bo had never helped carry his share. Eunice was older, but surely a boy seven years old could do a little bit.

Eunice heard somebody go running up the kitchen steps. That was no doubt Mama hastening away to hide. She would cower in the kitchen while Papa switched. She could not bear to watch.

The switching didn't hurt much. Papa was careful to touch her legs lightly because he knew he was making Mama equally wretched.

Injustice, however, was stinging Eunice. "Bo is the one. Bo is the one. He never brings his share," she wailed as she danced to the switch.

Sister Mattie had been gone for a week now. Sister Mattie would have run out and remonstrated with Papa. She would have stormed and argued and made Papa understand that Eunice's rebellion deserved support.

Now nobody took up for Eunice. Mama couldn't. She felt obliged to hold still when Papa punished since she could never bring herself to undertake any punishment at all. The young folks remaining at home were all too interested in their own affairs. At the supper table they ignored her and teased each other—mostly about sweethearts.

"Sister Mary! How would you like to have Lickskillet for your address?" Lately Dr. Ellis Whiter had been coming up from Lickskillet once a month to pay his respects.

"Ho! I think her address is more apt to be Nanafalia!" Earl Compton was coming from Nanafalia even more often.

Then Brother Ellis asked, "Sister Nora, do you think you'll ever peel *your* collection down to just two?"

At this everyone shrieked. Nora had too many sweethearts to count.

Brother Bunyan threw back his head and laughed as he said, "Sister Nora, I saw you crocheting on that 'fascinator' today." Bunyan thought it very funny of women to call head shawls fascinators. "Who are you setting your cap for now?"

"Not cap," Nora retorted. "Fascinator."

There were only two quiet ones at the table. One was a foot peddler who spoke little English. The other was Eunice. Eunice glanced over at that Bo. He was swinging his feet and blissfully eating his third helping. Somehow being the baby of a large family seemed to free him from all the obligations and rules which so rigidly bound the older ones.

Eunice could see no hope. She continued to fret inwardly. "I won't stand for it. Bo can't treat me this way. Papa can't treat me this way." Then she resolved, "I'm going to leave home. I'm going up to Choctaw Corner and live with Sister Mattie."

After supper the foot peddler began to open the great pack he carried on his back. It was made of black oilcloth and had leather straps fashioned to hold it across his shoulders. Inside was a selection of dry goods. There were yard goods in winter weights and colors, buttons, thread, fancy cotton bedspreads, doilies, dresser scarfs and tasseled lambrequins for draping mantelpieces and pianos. Mama, Sister Mary, and Sister Nora were swept away. They wanted everything. But the peddler knew so little English that he could barely make them understand his prices. He held up his fingers and waved his arms.

While they were all absorbed in the bargaining, Eunice slipped away. She found herself a piece of brown paper and a string and went quietly to her trunk in the shed room. She made a selection of her clothes and tied them in a bundle. Then she tucked the bundle in the bottom of the trunk under the tray so that it would not be in sight when the trunk was open.

She didn't know exactly how she would get to Mattie's. She could walk the nine miles, but she would see people who knew her even if she stayed off the road. But there'd be some way. Maybe she could ask a ride of a stranger. That thought brought the answer to her. Some of the peddlers came by in covered wagons. Why couldn't she sneak into one and hide? There was bound to be one soon. She remembered Mama saying this morning, "This sifter is worn out. I surely need a new one. High time the tin peddler came by. He usually makes it about this time of year." The tin peddler would be perfect. He always came in a covered wagon.

❧ *ten*

Tin Peddler

The bugle call echoed through the salmon-red clay hills. "Tin peddler, Eunice, tin peddler! Stop quick. Mama be hunting us and having a fit."

The tin peddler, still probably no closer than Glover, a mile away, blew his long, shiny tin bugle so that the women would have time to get their chickens and eggs ready to trade with him for his wares. His covered wagon was full of gleaming cake pans, sifters, kettles, boilers, graters, and tin cups. He was a welcome sight to the housewives because there were precious few towns between Mobile and Selma, and even ten miles to Thomasville was a long way to go on a horse or in a buggy.

"Run, Eunice! I can find enough chickens in the hen house, but I need you and Boland to go out and find some guinea eggs." Hunting guinea eggs was a hateful job which always fell to the children. There was never any telling where the guineas would lay their eggs. They'd scratch deep holes in the ground under a little bush pine out in the field. Sometimes there'd be thirty-five or forty eggs in a nest. Papa, Eunice, and Bo raced toward home.

"We're coming, Mama! We're coming!" They stayed in the backyard only long enough to snatch up a basket apiece. With the exciting notes from the bugle filling the air it was not so hard to june around and find nests. Eunice ran to each little pine that had sprouted up in the pasture. Her basket grew heavy.

She was glad that everybody was breathless from rushing around whenever the peddler came. She didn't want them to suspect that she had much more reason to be excited than they. Days had passed but she had not wavered in her resolve to go live with Mattie. My, would Mattie be glad to see her! She'd run out to meet her and hold her tight and say, "Oh, Eunice, never go back. I will never be homesick again if only you'll stay with me. We never, never should have been parted. Oh, how I have missed you, missed you!"

In the bustle nobody noticed Eunice's dash to the shed room where she flung open her trunk and brought out the paper bundle containing the clothes she had chosen to take. She concealed the bundle in the woodpile by the road near the peddler's usual stopping place.

The covered wagon was now in sight. The bugle music was the most beautiful Eunice had ever heard. Her family had had only jews' harps, harmonicas, and guitars, and some of the neighbors had accordions and violins. She had never seen an organ or a piano. The tin bugle was the best, and as it flashed in the sun, the peddler seemed to her a herald on a royal coach.

The bugle's purpose was twofold: the housewives were not only to prepare to barter, but also arrange to hold off the dogs and unlatch the gate. It seemed to the poor peddler that there was a dog barking under every crepe myrtle bush and chinaberry tree in Clarke County.

The guineas began a frenzied alarm as he drew near: *Pot rack, pot rack, pot rack, pot rack.* "Hold Major, Boland. Eunice, you unlatch the gate."

This time the peddler was a tall gaunt Scandinavian with scraggly, light colored hair and dirty teeth more than an inch long. He looked at the guineas and asked, "Vot kind of chicken iss dat?"

"A guinea fowl. The eggs are smaller but just as good."
But Mama was interested in the shiny wares. "What size coffee pots do you have? And while you're pulling things out, I'd like to see a sifter and a foot tub."

The peddler brought in the items Mama wanted to see. When he had them spread out, Eunice disappeared behind the woodpile by the road. She snatched her paper bundle and whizzed around the far side of the wagon. It was not hard to swing her lithe little body into the back of the wagon.

But, oh, the noise when she landed in the tin pans. The peddler thought his horse had moved and caused the clatter. "Ho dere. Ho. Ho," he called to the horse.

Several Rhode Island Red chickens somebody had traded lay there with their legs tied together. She stepped on one. "Squawk. Squawk. Squawk."

"Ohhhhhhhh. I'll be caught now for sure," thought Eunice. How could she ever squinch down in the shadows among those pans and chickens and eggs without making a clatter? The best looking spot appeared to be between a solid stack of pie plates, two deep, and a stack of dishpans. There was something between them but it wasn't high; she could probably sit on it. She sat, but it didn't take long to realize that what she was sitting on was a pile of graters.

Mama was asking, "How much credit for eggs, fryers, and hens today?" The peddler allowed her ten cents a dozen for eggs, ten cents for a fryer, fifteen cents for hens. He could take them to Thomasville and get a little more.

Mama and the peddler came to an agreement. Through it all Boland held onto Major and waited for just one thing. As the peddler climbed to his seat, he begged breathlessly, "Could we have another blow?"

The peddler blew a bugle call. My, it was loud up close! Eunice thought, as the wagon creaked off with tin wares banging and chickens squawking. "I just must find something else to sit on. I can't stand these graters very long."

For a moment she wished somebody would run down the road and shout, "Stop! We want back our Eunice!"

But nobody did. Even with Bud Nap, Bud, Sister Maggie, and now Sister Mattie gone, there were still twelve people left at the immediate homestead, and nobody was considered missing unless he failed to appear at a meal. It was only 1:30 in the afternoon. Unless she were wanted for a particular chore, it would probably be five or six o'clock before anyone realized she was gone.

The wagon was smelly. The peddler did not bother to clean it between trips. It smelled like a henhouse. The eggbeaters, which looked so new and sparkling in the sun, were shoddily made when you stared at them.

The next stop was at Old Man Johnson's house. She prayed, "Dear Lord, don't let Old Mrs. Johnson need a pie pan or a dishpan."

Mrs. Johnson needed only a long stirring spoon. Eunice held her knees against her while the peddler rummaged. He was slow, and Mrs. Johnson was slower. Eunice decided that her Mama certainly could get things done in a hurry.

She held her breath at the Clark's and again at the Hill's. Each stop took a long time. Next was the Williams'. Eunice could hear Newell chattering to Carlos. She caught one sentence. "Carlos, if you get some corn bread and onion, bring me some, too."

Corn bread and onion. Best thing in the world between meals. "Oh, Newell, if you just knew that I am in here being grated and about to starve."

It was a miracle the way the peddler happened to avoid seeing her as he snatched for different things.

The next place on the way was Uncle John Griffin's. The house sat so far back from the road that the peddler turned left and drove up the little lane that led to it. Eunice recognized every rut and jog. No telling how many times she and Bo had ridden Old Cap here. Now they were passing the peach trees where she had sat and gorged herself last summer. Suddenly she thought of Cousin Omer. Oh, that Omer with his hot pepper! She was glad, glad to be leaving this part of the country. She wouldn't be in school with him from now on. Ho! Wouldn't it surprise Omer if she should step from the wagon cover and pick up that bugle and give it a blow? And just sit up there like a stranger and stare straight ahead and not know him?

But that mean boy didn't come to see the peddler. The voices were those of her staunch friend, Cousin Lily, and easygoing Aunt Lyddie. Wouldn't a drink of Aunt Lyddie's buttermilk feel good on her parched throat now? Aunt Lyddie was peculiar not to be willing to sleep on a bed made by somebody else, but, oh, she was so kind. My, but she'd have a good time if she hopped out here. She'd be welcome to stay a week. Eat Aunt Lyddie's biscuits, play dolls with Lily. It could be wonderful.

But Tah-deet-tah-deet-tah-deeeeeeee. The tin bugle split the air, and off they rolled again. It was growing dark inside the wagon now. The sunlight had faded. At the next stop the peddler had to grope for a dishpan, and by keeping her head down Eunice easily avoided him.

It was getting dark and she was getting hungry. She had played the fool by bringing clothes to wear but nothing to eat. She could just hear Mama saying, "Child, you don't have a bit of foresight." But food was so bountiful at home that it was the last thing Eunice would have dreamed that she might ever be without.

There was one more house and store, St. David, where the Whites lived, and then not another house the whole four miles to Choctaw Corner. Usually the peddler spent the night and ate at somebody's house in exchange for his tin wares. Eunice prayed that he would decide to ride through the darkness to get home rather than ask shelter from the Whites. He stopped at St. David, all right, and he watered his horse.

She thought, "Suppose he spends the night at the Whites. I'm already getting cold, and I'd be hungry, too. The mule and chickens would be watered and fed, but not me. And there's no room to stretch out and really rest."

But after awhile the peddler climbed back on his seat and began crunching crackers. She smelled cheese. He must have decided to go on home to Thomasville. Relieved, she settled back for the long jolting ride in the dark.

But she soon began to fret again. How would she get off at Choctaw Corner? Could she see houses in the dark? Which one was Mattie's? How would she know when it would be time to get there? Could she clamber over all those chickens and eggs? She had never dropped off a wagon until it stopped—would she get hurt jumping down from a moving wagon? When they got a good way from the Whites, might she just as well confess to the peddler that he had a stowaway? Oh, maybe not. It would be too hard to talk to him. He spoke just enough English to sell and barter. She could never make him understand.

In all her life Eunice had never had to decide so many things for herself. All of this part of the road was strange to her; she had never been up here even once in daytime. She had repeated to herself many times Mattie's last words to Papa. "Remember: it's the first two-story house with a fenced lane leading back to it. Sits way back from the road. A pear grove on each side." Now the instructions raced through her mind over and over again. Was she remembering right?

The moon came up. It was not a full brilliant one, but it gave enough light to make it possible to see shadowy outlines. The moonlight brought home to Eunice the fact that finding Mattie's would have been out of the question if the night had been rainy or cloudy. My, what a chance she had heedlessly taken. Eunice gradually wormed her way up to the center of the back of the wagon. By organizing the eggs and chickens a little better, she made herself a sitting place. The peddler must have thought his chickens restless, but Eunice was brazen now.

It seemed to Eunice that hours went by. No houses. Just woods and fields, woods and fields. No bugle playing. The lonely peddler began to sing to himself. He sang one old Swedish song after another. Eunice loved them. The rhythms made her want to whirl and stomp. Poor homesick peddler. All alone across the ocean from home. Eunice would have liked to have sat up there on the seat by him and laughed and clapped her hands to the tunes. Instead she swayed from side to side and thought, "Bo would love to be hearing these with me." She straightened in alarm at herself. She must remember to be thankful she was leaving that aggravating child.

At last she saw a church steeple against the moonlit sky. Papa had been so pleased that Mattie could go to the Methodist church in Choctaw Corner. They passed a house. Another. Another. None of those three had a fenced lane. Neither did the next. But, look, they had just passed a fenced lane, and yes, the house up the hill from it had two stories. She eased and eased herself to the very edge of the wagon, dangled her toes as low as possible, and let go. The jar she felt through her shoes went right up to her head, but she wasn't hurt. The paper bundle had rustled. She stayed still in a shadow for a minute in case the peddler investigated the noise.

Then she darted up the lane and ran. Oh, but it was pitch dark under those trees. This certainly must be the right house. The trees in the groves on each side were scraggly and shapeless like pear trees.

It was so dark that she felt her way up the steps on her hands and knees. Not a lamp burning. So late they'd gone to bed. She banged and called, "Sister Mattie! Sister Mattie!"

She stomped her feet. "Sister MATTIE. Whoo-hoo-*Mattie*. *Oh,* Sister Mattie."

No answer. Suppose they were not at home? Oh, my, suppose this were not the right house after all. She shouted, "*SISTER MATTIE.*"

There were noises inside. Then a lamp was lit and Brother Marion called, "Who's there?"

"It's me—Eunice."

"*Who*"

"Eunice—Mattie's sister."

"Eunice!"

Sister Mattie appeared and echoed, "Eunice!"

They fussed sleepily with the door latch. The door opened and she saw them in their night clothes. Brother Marion held the lamp and peered at her. "What on earth are you doing here, Eunice?"

"I caught a ride up with the tin peddler. I thought I'd like to come and stay with you."

"Eunice, do you mean that Mama and Papa let you ride up here with that peddler and be out in the night like this?"

"Well, no, I just caught a ride with the peddler. I hid in his wagon. They don't know yet."

"*Don't know*! Eunice! Mama and Papa and nobody on the place will sleep a wink tonight. They're probably already combing the woods."

Eunice's thoughts spun and came to a standstill focusing on those back at home. That part had never occurred to her. She had been so busy running away successfully that she had never thought about how it would affect Mama and Papa until they knew where she was.

"Well, come on in here and let's get on some clothes and decide what to do." This was not at all what Eunice had visualized. Sister Mattie was supposed to clasp her tight and

80

declare that she had missed her every moment and that she wanted her to live there always.

Sister Mattie did give her a quick fierce hug, but she had a troubled look in her eyes. "Eunice, it's wonderful, wonderful to see you, but it shouldn't be like this. I'm so glad you've been thinking of me, but you have to think about the others, too. Mama and Papa, Mary and Nora, Ellis, Bunyan, Fowler, Woodley, Cephas—I can see them all now just crazy with worry."

"Oh, they don't care about me. That's why I came to stay with you."

"Care! Eunice! That family of ours is strong on poking fun and very clumsy at showing affection, but you must never think for a minute that they don't all love you. Oh, poor Mama! I know she has held her breath ever since you didn't show up at the supper table. Surely you didn't realize, Eunice; surely you didn't plan to upset the family . . ."

No, she had not planned to hurt Mama! In her grief and resentment she had thought of nobody but herself. All she had planned was a way of getting to Mattie. She had indeed been thoughtless. And, oh, she was hungry now. So hungry she hardly felt right. "Sister Mattie?"

"Yes?"

"Sister Mattie, have y'all had supper?"

"Heavenly days! We've had supper and gone to bed. But *you* haven't, have you? Of course not. Come on back here."

She unlatched the back hall door, and they trailed single file over the walk to the kitchen. Their footsteps on the planks sounded loud in the still night. Sister Mattie began uncovering buttermilk, cold chicken, corn bread, and black-eyed peas. Brother Marion paced.

"Mattie, no point in waiting 'til morning. Your folks are no doubt half wild by now. I may just as well saddle up and ride down there now as wait 'til morning. Take the load off their minds. I'll stay down there and get some rest, and later on tomorrow one of the boys can ride up with me to take Eunice home. Good thing this is a Saturday night."

It didn't even seem to occur to Brother Marion that she might live with them. He left. She sat at the table mechanically poking down a few bites and swallows. Hungry as she was, nothing tasted good.

❦ ❦ ❦

The next morning Eunice hustled around helping to do Brother Marion's chores. With just two of them there was a lot more work to do than at home. But even with all that workload Sister Mattie didn't show any sign of inviting her to stay for good. Now Eunice began to dread going home and facing the family.

Early that afternoon Brother Ellis arrived in the buggy to carry her home. Weary Brother Marion was alongside on his horse. "Why, Eunice," Brother Ellis said gently as he hopped down and tied the horse. "The idea. Didn't you know some of us would bring you to see Mattie? Knowing how you miss her, nobody'd think of going to Thomasville without offering to drop you off here."

Sister Mattie shyly embraced Brother Marion. "Oh, poor Mr. Kimbrough. And poor Brother Ellis, to have to ride all the way up here and back all at once. Do come in long enough for some cake and milk."

"Eunice, your mother was sick with worry. Downright sick."

"I'll say. She couldn't help look for you any more after we found out you weren't at the Days' or Grandma's or the Williams' or Uncle John's. She just lay down on her bed, staring at the wall. Aunt Lyddie stayed with her, praying, down on her knees by the bed."

Eunice was stunned. Mama taking to her bed, and Aunt Lyddie praying. How right Mattie had been.

"Everybody was out hunting you. I mean everybody. When folks heard, they just threw down and set out just the way they were. There was Mr. Os Hill, it pitch dark, ten o'clock at night, and him out still wearing that eyeshade. He took Earl and Carl Day with him to check that old abandoned well near the Big Gully."

Eunice drew in her breath with surprise.

"You should have seen it, Sister Mattie. For miles around lanterns flashing like june bugs. Everybody was imagining what had happened to Eunice. Bo thought maybe a vine swing had broken, and she'd fallen and was too hurt to move. Mr. Williams saw a wildcat last week, and, of course, you know how Grandpa Holland still remembers the days when there were wolves and bears. We still can't convince him they've all disappeared."

Brother Ellis reached for another piece of cake, and Brother Marion took up the story. "When I got there with the news, your Papa went out to the top of the hill and built a big bonfire. That was the signal to stop searching. But Mr. Jarvis was practically to Bashi by then, and Uncle John was past Tallahatta Springs, so neither one of them saw it. It was about daylight before we caught up with them."

By now Eunice was sunk in guilt. She hadn't used her imagination! She had used her imagination forward but not backwards. She had visualized only her welcome by Mattie and hadn't considered for a moment what would be happening at home when she didn't appear at the supper table.

Right then she wished these three wouldn't hold their tempers so well. They made her feel even more ashamed of herself. It'd be easier if they'd storm at her like Sister Nora or be as blunt as little Bo.

"Mighty good pound cake, Sister Mattie. Hate to eat and rush off, but I expect we'd better start on." As Mattie walked out to the buggy with them she sensed that Eunice needed no further rebukes. What Eunice needed now was a goal to sustain her through the reception she would get at home.

She put her arm around her. "You know, Eunice, Mr. Kimbrough did so enjoy teaching you. You were a perfect delight to him. He has been saying that when you finish that little school near home, he thinks it would be nice for you to come and stay with us so you can go to a fine school. Three or four years from now. We'd love you now, but Mama could never bear to part with you while you're this young, and you need her, too. But you work hard and do well in school, and Mama and Papa will want you to go on. Maybe you'll be the one of all us girls to go to college at the Judson up in Marion. Think of that!"

 *eleven*

Playing Lady at Grandma Holland's

Winter came and went, and now spring was here.

"This is the last of the stuffed sausage. I want Grandma and Grandpa Holland to have some. They don't have a bit left." Mama placed a portion of the sausage in a basket. Then she began carefully filling the remainder of the basket with strawberries.

"Their strawberries are not bearing yet. Let's give them some of ours. Run here, Eunice! Boland! I want you two to get on Old Cap and take these things to Grandma Holland." Now here was a pleasant errand. They had been planning to walk over anyway if they could just finish their chores.

Bo looked up and Papa's eye caught his. Without a word he went for Old Cap and bridled him. Nothing had ever been said, but Bo now sensed that there were times when he'd better help. He didn't even stop to joke with Papa about the possibility of riding Midnight.

"Eunice, while Bo's bringing Old Cap you'd better run get your sun hat. Not too early in the year for you to get freckled and burned."

Eunice fetched a stool to reach down her hat from the rack. "Yunnis, is that a hat?" rung in her ears. But she jammed the hat down on her head and forgot about it because Bo was back with Old Cap. She mounted in front and took hold of the reins and the fishing poles. Mama handed Bo the big basket and said, "You can stay and spend the night with Grandma if you want to. Eunice, if you do stay, just one thing. Tell her to pin a searcloth on Boland's chest tonight. I don't like the way that cough of his is hanging on. Small wonder. He got barefooted this year before the ground warmed up."

As they set off Papa said drily, "Now don't you two give The Whip any trouble."

The Whip again. Eunice asked, "Papa, *why* do you call Grandma that?"

As usual Papa grinned but did not answer. "Bo, do you see why? I keep asking Papa and he won't answer me."

"She's long and skinny like a whip."

"She is. But I don't think that's enough of a reason. Lots of people are long and skinny."

Grandma Holland's house was several miles away when you stayed on the road. Up the long red clay hills. Down the long red clay hills. There were white blossoms on the dewberry and blackberry bushes which nestled beneath the tall pines on each side of the road.

"Um. Ummmm. Smell!"

"Smells good."

"Must be a sloe tree. 'Bout the best smelling one of all." Sure enough, around the curve was a big sloe tree, covered with pinkish white blossoms. It was nice to be high up on Old Cap's back and ride so close underneath the fragrant boughs.

On and on they went. They didn't see a single person the whole way, but the roadside was alive with rabbit, squirrel, and bird families. And the one good thing about Cap being so slow was that you didn't miss seeing a thing.

Grandma's house was up on a high hill. The lower part of the hill was covered with cowcumber trees. At this time of year the trees bore their giant magnolia-like blooms. Grandma happened to look out a side window and caught a glimpse of them as they passed a pasture on their way. She turned and called to old Aunt Mary, her faithful servant, "Here come Eunice and Boland! Count them in for dinner, Mary."

Then she walked out to the gate to meet the children. Old Cap's slow plod halted. "What's all this? Strawberries already? Yes, your patch gets so much more sun than ours. And sausage! Lou managed to keep some this late! My, such a treat! Hers is so much better than mine ever was. Here, take Cap to the barnyard and hurry on in. Dinner's about ready."

Right after dinner Mamie Burge came over to play. Mamie was an orphan who lived on the next farm with her aunt, Miss Mandy Walker. She had glimpsed Bo and Eunice as they rode Old Cap up the hill to the barn. In her haste to come over and join them she had gobbled her dinner down without tasting it.

Grandma meanwhile slipped away to her room to resume work on her sewing. She was working on the trousseau of the daughter of some big rich folks in Marengo County. The children followed her. They eyed the hoops hanging on the wall. Hoops hadn't been worn since a few years after the war, but Grandma had never bothered to get rid of them. "The way styles come and go, you never can tell. Who knows, girls, you may be wearing them yourselves some day."

"Let us wear them today, Grandma."

"You want to?"

Grandma reached up for a set of hoops for each of them. The hoops were circles of steel wire encased in cotton cloth. They were attached by cloth tapes running lengthwise. Such a tangle! To get them on was like solving a puzzle. Mamie and Eunice succeeded, but Bo's looked messier than it had to begin with. He was laughing and scrambling. They exclaimed with annoyance, "Bo! You're making yours even worse than it really is." Bo laughed even harder. He knew he was guilty.

As they straightened him out Grandma opened a trunk and brought out three skirts. They were relics of days before the war and were sumptuous. They were rotten and threadbare now, but it was easy to see why Grandma couldn't resist keeping a few.

She gave Mamie one of rose silk. The lower skirt was of striped rose and mauve with a pleated ruffle around the bottom. The upper skirt had a narrower ruffle and was festooned with black velvet ribbons. To Eunice fell a mauve silk with wide black lace around the bottom. It was plain in front, but very, very full in back, and as she finished putting it on she exclaimed with pleasure, "Look! It has a train!"

"Well, not a long train like a queen might wear, Eunice, but it is what they call a demi-train. Of course, you being small, it *is* a long train for you."

Next Bo. His was of steel gray taffeta with pink satin rosettes at intervals. In the center of each rosette was a cluster of artificial green grapes with green leaves!

Out into the yard they paraded. Mamie's heart was bursting. Miss Mandy did well to keep her in calico and gingham, and never had she had such a taste of glory. Eunice was equally in a dream world. She'd doubted that she'd ever wear a train even on her wedding day. She held her whole body erect and raised her chin. Such a regal gown demanded regal carriage.

Mamie and Eunice strutted, but Bo stood still, doubled over. Those artificial grapes. He couldn't resist feeling them. He had seen a lot of feminine frippery at home, but this was the wildest ever. He giggled and giggled. "Grandma! Grandma! How are you supposed to *sit down* on grapes?"

About this time Mamie suddenly stopped, pointing to one of the cowcumber trees. "I know what! let's make cowcumber parasols to go with our skirts!"

That was easy. Cowcumber leaves grow more than a yard long and a half yard wide. The three children each broke off a limb. Then they pinned the leaves on the limb together with thorns from a thorn bush, making enormous parasols. The parasols gave fresh impetus to strutting. Grandpa's newly sheared lambs frisked around the three children. It was a spring festival.

Then Eunice contributed an idea. "We could make hats!"

"Hats!"

"Hats! Wait 'til you see mine. Hee. Hee."

Down came more cowcumber leaves. And, sure enough, the leaves gradually turned into stylish hats trimmed with violets, wild roses, and wild azaleas. Bo had fits of laughter as he made his. He kept saying, "Look. Look. It's exactly like the hat SiBary wears to church. Exactly! Now, ain't it? See? See? Flowers sticking up in the front and flowers sticking up in the back!"

Making the hats and parasols was so satisfying that they decided to shed the skirts Grandma had given them and make their own. The giant leaves could easily be laid over the hoops to make skirts. Bo and Mamie began tearing their leaves and pinning them on any old which-a-way.

But not Eunice. In her mind's eye was one of those Butterick patterns Sister Mary had ordered from the *Delineator*. She had watched Mary cut it out, fit it, and sew on it between times during the past two weeks. She had turned the machine to make nearly every stitch in it. Now she deserted the others and went running into the house. "Grandma, would you let me borrow your worst old scissors?"

"Look on the kitchen table. I last used them to cut liners for cake pans."

Eunice found the scissors and, after a quick stop by the can of molasses cake, she ran out to join the others. She decided to shed her hoops. Then she began work on the skirt. She made a fold up and down the front. In the center of the back she carefully folded two box plaits. She used two leaves in front and three in back, meticulously pinning them together with thorns.

Next she attempted a cape like Mary's. It wasn't really so hard, because the small end of cowcumber leaves in halves provided a tight fit around the shoulders, and the middles made it flare out just below the waist. To finish the cape she even pinned three fastening tabs across the front, and with an extra leaf added a hood hanging down the back, just the way the pattern was designed.

Mamie and Bo were ready now and watched her pin the last tab. The three carefully glided back to the house, pausing occasionally to replace a lost thorn pin.

"Grandma! Grandpa! Aunt Mary! Come out on the gallery and look at us." The old folks were delighted. Bo and Mamie were quaint little old-timey ladies. But it was Eunice's up-to-date suit that caused Grandma to get a piercing look in her eyes.

Eunice saw it and confessed promptly. "I copied the suit Mary's just made."

Grandma commanded sharply. "Turn around, Eunice. Now turn sideways. Now let me look at the front again."

Then she sat down in a rocker as if she had to. "Mr. Holland," she said softly, "Mr. Holland, look at the way she has cut and fitted it. Why, the child is a born dressmaker. I'm going to tell her mother that it isn't a bit too soon to give her a piece of cloth."

Then to Eunice she said, "Eunice! You deserve first prize. Why, I'd trust you to make me a shirtwaist right now."

As soon as the judging was over, the fine ladies began prancing their fragile leaf dresses into shreds. Mamie sailed her parasol through the air. She ran after a lamb until she caught him, and then she forced her hat down on his head.

Then she returned from her make-believe world with a start. "Oh! It's getting late and I have to go!"

"Well, if you're real sure you have to, we'll walk piece o' way home with you."

Eunice and Boland politely walked all the way to Miss Mandy's pasture gate with Mamie because there would be the two of them to come back together. That is, Eunice and Mamie walked together while Bo tagged behind, occasionally gaining attention by his customary "Hooo-ooo. Hoooooo-ooooooo. Won't wait for me."

Yet Mamie looked at Eunice enviously as she waved goodbye. All those sisters and brothers and in-laws and aunts and uncles and cousins and grandpas and grandmas! She and Miss Mandy only had each other. Eunice sensed Mamie's envy. On the way back she didn't mind so much having to stop and stop and stop to wait for Bo to catch up.

"Grandma, we can spend the night."

"Fine. Be glad to have you. After all, we moved over here from Dixons Mill to be near Lou and Ivey and you children."

There were chicken and dumplings for supper as well as some of the stuffed sausage. For dessert they had the strawberries in heavy cream. Then when they left the table, Grandma brought out a great pan of peanuts she had parched in the oven. They all sat around shelling and eating them.

Grandma and Grandpa knew of several real ghosts. Bo and Eunice wanted to hear about them, even though they had heard the stories time and again. Grandma told them just as carefully and made them just as scary as if she were telling them for the first time. Eunice and Boland were rigid with terror when the clock struck seven and Grandma stopped suddenly, saying, "Time for you two to get ready for bed."

Then Eunice remembered what Mama had said that morning. "Grandma, Mama says to put a searcloth on Boland because of his cough."

"Child, haven't you smelled it? I already have one out in the kitchen warming."

When Eunice and Bo ran and jumped into bed, Grandma brought in the searcloth. It was a square of worn, soft, outing flannel, soaked in kerosene oil and smeared with tallow to keep the oil from burning the skin. Grandma had used it for years. Just sprinkled on a little more kerosene and added a bit of tallow each time. As she pinned it inside Boland's shirt so it would cover his chest, the odor penetrated the entire room. "Hee. Hee. Hee." The rag tickled.

Then Grandma fed Boland a teaspoonful of sugar with a few drops of olive tar on it.

When she left them Eunice snuggled down and wondered aloud, "Now, Bo, why is it that at home you're not important or special, but at somebody else's house you are?"

❀ twelve

A Squirrel, a Catfish, and the Whip

All that spring Sister Mattie made a special effort to come home often enough to make Eunice and the rest of the family feel that she had not deserted them.

Summer came, but it brought little difference in routine. School, as always, flowed right on through the summer months. Suddenly it was the last Sunday in August. Bo said, "Mama, we're going over to Grandma Holland's to fish."

"Not until after dinner. Don't you realize that it's about time right now? You children can ring the dinner bell for me."

Soon everybody was at his place at the table. No, not everybody. Brother Ellis was late. He was usually the late one. There was always an extra bit of attention he wanted to give Midnight. Papa didn't like to ask the blessing until everybody was present. As they squirmed and the food grew cold and the flies began to zoom, even Mama grew impatient. Brother Ellis finally came in the door.

"This happens entirely too often. Even if Midnight is with foal that is no excuse whatever for you to be late for dinner," said Mama.

"Foal? Midnight?"

"You didn't tell *us*. We didn't know!" This was news indeed to Eunice and Bo.

"Wait now. Wait now. Just wait. We haven't told you younger children before because we didn't want to excite you so far ahead. The colt won't be here until December."

"Papa. Papa. Are you going to let us ride this one?"

Papa raised his hand with a silencing gesture. "Ootchie. Boland. Now you two just quiet down. Quiet down. There'll be many a day before anybody can ride that horse."

They held in during the rest of the meal. There was sugary-crusted muscadine pie, and that was good enough to help them be quiet.

After dinner Eunice stayed back with the womenfolks to help with the dishes while the menfolks went on up front. But she soon heard Papa calling her. "Ootchie. Ootchie. Run here. Somebody to see you."

Eunice sped around the house to the front yard. When she saw her visitor she stopped stone still. It was Mr. Os Hill.

Mr. Os Hill. She was mystified. If somebody she knew only as a character in history or in a book had called on her she would not have been more surprised. His buggy was headed toward Thomasville, and he was all dressed up. Then suddenly a furry little rusty head peered out of his pocket. It was a squirrel. Why, it was Lucy, Miss Nin's pet squirrel! "Eunice, I stopped by to offer you Lucy. Sister Nin's not feeling well these days and has decided to get rid of her. We both thought of you because you seemed to like her the day you saw her in the store."

To think of owning Lucy! Eunice ran forward and took her happily. Lucy hopped up onto her shoulder and sat there. She seemed completely satisfied.

Mr. Os explained further. "Sister Nin feels less frisky every day that passes, and Lucy gets more frisky every day that passes. And Lucy has gotten so she nips Nin now and then. Sister Nin is of the opinion that she needs a mistress who is younger and can dodge faster."

"I can dodge. I can dodge fast. Oh, Mr. Os, I do thank you and Miss Nin. I do want Lucy." Suddenly she became aware of the responsibility of ownership. "Oh! Mr. Os, do you feed her anything besides the nuts she finds for herself?"

"Oh, yes. Give her bread crumbs and meat scraps, and she'll enjoy them." He turned, slowly and grandly, in the direction of the well. "And now, if you two are happy with each other, I'll help myself to a dipper of water and be on my way to Thomasville." Somehow Mr. Os could act important even as he drank a dipper of water. He reared back and drained the last drop. "Ahhhhhhhh." Good. Fine well you folks have."

He didn't just scramble back up into his buggy like other people. He mounted slowly and majestically. Before he loosened the reins, he tipped his hat to Eunice.

Back on the gallery Sister Nora and Sister Mary released their giggles. "Whooooooo! Does he put on airs!" But Eunice didn't feel that way any more. She liked him. All his pompousness had not concealed his essential friendliness. Somehow she now felt sure that Mr. Os must have liked her all along, too, even though he had made fun of her.

Bo brought her back from her thoughts. "Eunice. Eunice. Let me hold Lucy awhile. Please." Lucy snuggled down on Bo's arm. The children marveled. Never had they managed to get a squirrel to be very friendly. How had Miss Nin done it?

Bo remembered their fishing plans. "Lucy goin' fishin' with us?" Bo had just started digging for bait when Mr. Os had come. He and Eunice were planning to do their fishing over at Grandma and Grandpa Holland's and then spend the night with them. Now Lucy scurried around them as they dug for worms in Papa's freshly plowed field.

Bo said hopefully, "Ought to be some big fellers turned up out here." There were. They filled their can with inviting fat worms and were soon hurrying over to the creek near Grandma's to give their luck a try. Why they were so eager was a mystery. In years of fishing they had never caught a fish longer than four inches.

Today they did not lack for something to chatter about on the way. Think of that colt they would have next December. Why, it was bound to be fine and beautiful like Midnight. Surely Papa would give in on this one and let them ride him. And think of Miss Nin and Mr. Os giving them Lucy. They could hardly believe that she was still right here with them. Was there ever such a squirrel?

When they reached the little stream Bo picked a good spot. Then he left it. "No. I'm goin' on down a-piece. Changed my mind."

Before Eunice settled down she called Lucy from a tree overhead just to make sure Lucy would answer her. She ran down the tree trunk and paused on the log at Eunice's feet. Now that she felt that Lucy was secure she stood at the spot Bo had rejected.

"Such a worm," Eunice thought as she baited her hook. "My, this one ought to look good to them." She threw out her line with assurance. Not long afterward there was a strong tug. She pulled hard. Up came a catfish more than a foot long.

But it was a fighter. Eunice thought, "Never, never have I had a real fish on my line. I *will* land him. I *will*." She planted her feet firmly and then turned sideways, flinging the frantic fish onto the bank. It flipped and flopped and squirmed and slithered.

Bo came running. "Hold him, Eunice. Hold him."

"Help get him off the hook, Bo. Help." But the two of them together could not get the fish off that hook. It was as though the fish knew they were only children and was doubly determined not to be conquered.

Eunice saw they were making no progress. "Let go, Bo. Quit trying."

She snatched up the line and ran like a spirit up the hill to the house where Grandpa was sitting on the vine shaded gallery. When Grandpa saw Eunice coming, he rose from his chair and started down the steps to meet her. "Grandpa! Grandpa! Grandpa!"

He seized the line and swiftly slipped the fish off the hook. Then he grasped it firmly by the tail and held it high. Examining it, he marveled, "This is without a doubt the biggest fish ever caught in that little stream. Eunice, shall we get your Grandma to cook it and give it to us for supper?"

Eunice did not answer. She could not make herself say so, but she was wishing she could take it home and show it off to Papa and Mama and all the older brothers and sisters.

But sure enough, Grandpa did clean the fish, and Aunt Mary dipped it in cornmeal and fried it. Grandma also fried two chickens, but she served them as a mere side dish. Bo took a bit of the fish. So crisp outside and so soft and meaty and mild inside. "Good."

" 'Deed it is good," Grandpa agreed. "In fact, it's a treat such as we haven't had in a long time. I'm getting entirely too old to go all the way to the Tombigbee to fish."

"Catfish!" Grandma sighed with pleasure. "Common a fish as it is, it's still a real delicacy, Eunice."

After supper they all went out to rock on the front gallery. Grandma was knitting summer work socks for Grandpa out of some of the cotton thread that Mary had spun during the winter. A pair of socks knitted from Mary's thread would last much longer than socks you might buy at a store. Lucy ran up and down the posts that supported the roof over the gallery.

Bo rocked with gusto and issued a command. "Tell about The War, Grandpa."

Grandpa beamed. This was a ritual. The way Grandma

never put fried chicken on the table without rice and gravy to go with it—well, that was the way Bo and Grandpa never rocked together without Bo's demanding a story about The War.

It was tedious to listen to some old folks talk, but not to Grandpa. He had been forty-five years old when the war started and didn't have to go, but he wouldn't have missed the excitement for the world. For his excuse he told Grandma he had to go along and look after Ivey. That was Papa. So, off he had gone with Papa and the other young men, leaving behind Grandma and Mama and Bud Nap, a small baby then.

Because Grandpa was so good at handling oxen, he had been put in charge of a wagon train of supplies for the Confederate Army. He could tell of journeys as far up as Louisville, Kentucky, and all up in Virginia, clear to Richmond.

"Grandpa, tell again about the great egg scrambling."

"Well, here's how it was, Boland. I never had any trouble with the oxen or wagons that I couldn't handle, but toward the end of the war it got so we had no provisions to haul. But the fighting boys were depending on us, so I'd get out and scrape and scrounge for just anything I could find anywhere.

"One time the men were so hungry they were about ready to give up. So hungry they were sick and some of them about crazy. So I just drove a wagon out in the country and went to every farm, big and little, for miles and miles around. I begged those folks to sell me every egg they could possibly spare. After all, I told them, I was not asking them for their chickens. Just their eggs. Well, they all had precious little for themselves, but that made sense to them. I managed to get a few from some and dozens from others. I kept on until at last I had that whole big supply wagon just heaped up with eggs.

"When I rode back into camp with that load of eggs, those hungry, mournful-looking boys just about went wild with joy. They got out and roamed around until they found a great big old cast-iron wash pot—just like the one we have here out back to boil the white clothes in—only four or five times as big. They built a good fire under it, and we began cracking it full of eggs. Such a cracking. Dozens and dozens and dozens of eggs. About six boys stood around the pot and started cracking eggs on the edge of it and plopping them down into the deep pot. Crack-plop. Crack-plop. Crack-plop. Think of it. We cracked that whole big wagon load of eggs down into that pot.

"Then we got ourselves a great big stick to scramble them with. We stirred and we scrambled and we salted, and we stirred and we scrambled and we salted some more, and when those eggs were done, I'm telling you they were the best tasting . . ."

But the rest of the story could not be heard for the din from out back. Something had wakened the chickens!

Cut cut cut cut cut-tut! Cut cut cut cut cut cut-tut! The hens were all cackling.

Without a word Grandma was in her room reaching down a rifle from above the mantelpiece and running out the back door with it. Eunice and Bo looked at each other, and each read the other's thought. Like a whip. Exactly. Grandma had uncurled and ripped by just that fast. She hadn't run or stumbled around at all the way other people would have. Just whipped out back. Now they knew why Papa called her the Whip!

Grandpa didn't even get up. "You children keep your seats. Just stay right where you are. Your Grandma'll tend to 'im. If it's a fox, she'll get him. If it's a man, she'll scare him so he'll never come back around here again as long as he lives."

Eunice and Bo remained speechless. Grandpa seemed to sense that they were wondering how it was that in this house Grandma seemed to be the one who chased off the prowlers. At home Papa was the one who went out.

"Oh, your Grandma always goes after 'em. Started that way when your Papa and I went off to the war and left her and your Mama and the baby here. Yes, Nap was just a new baby then. Your Grandma would say, 'Nobody's going to steal all I've worked for so hard. We cleared the timber off this land. We plowed it up and cultivated it. I've sewn a thousand dresses to help buy stock for it. I've fed and watered and looked after every living thing on this place. Now nobody, *nobody* is going to steal it from me.' And, sure enough, every time she heard a disturbance, out she went shooting. Got so in the habit she's never quit. Just leaps up, grabs the gun, and runs out the minute she hears a sound. I figure it's safer for me to stay still than to go out and complicate things with another gun."

Crack. Grandma had shot. Next thing they heard was Grandma calmly scraping her feet on the back steps. She came back in through the house, and as she replaced the gun in the rack over the mantelpiece, she announced in a matter of fact tone, "Fox. I'll let you drag him off in the morning, Mr. Holland."

When they waked the next day, Grandpa had already dragged the fox off to the woods. Bo was disappointed. "Aw. I wanted to help. I wanted to *see* that fox."

Both Grandpa and Grandma told him that they were sorry. Then Grandma consoled him with pancakes and pancakes and pancakes for breakfast. And later on when they called Lucy and started for home, Grandma gave them each a big piece of molasses cake to eat on the way.

Once out of hearing Eunice spoke her mind. "Bo, you think Grandpa must be so big because he was a wagon master in the war? Might be. But look at Grandma. Went out all by herself on dark nights to fight thieves and wild animals. Nobody commanding her to do it, either. She could have stayed inside all locked up. Those soldiers in the war had somebody commanding them to fight. And they had each other. There was always somebody else with a gun right alongside. But Grandma was miles from help." By now she had worked herself up to something that was bold to say, even to Bo. "*I think Grandma Holland is even a lot braver than Grandpa Holland.*"

❈ thirteen

Molasses Making

Papa flicked a crumb from his beard and pushed his chair back from the head of the table as they were all finishing breakfast. "I don't want anybody to forget that tomorrow is molasses making day. It's the last day of October, and that's as late as I'm going to wait. Let a frost come, and the cane will lose its sweetness and flavor. You all must june around here today and help see to it that every bit of that cane gets cut and topped and stripped. Tomorrow, Mr. Walker and Frank will come over and help us run the mill."

They all knew Papa meant business. A year's supply of molasses for a large family and all the wage-hands was a very important matter. Papa was particularly fond of good ribbon cane molasses and wanted a pitcher full in the middle of the table at every meal the year 'round.

As she rose from the table, Eunice leaned over and picked up the pewter pitcher. Bringing in the gallon stone pitcher full of molasses once a week was only part of her chore. She had to keep the little pitcher on the table filled. And every so often she had to take it out to the sandpile and polish it by applying sand with a corncob.

But this was no day for polishing. She hastily did the refill job which was always necessary after their breakfast of sausage and hot biscuits. She drew water from the well and brought it in, fed and watered the chickens, helped churn, fluffed and smoothed the feather beds, took up the oak ashes from the fireplaces and carried them out to the ash hopper. Today she would be excused from sweeping the yard.

Now, at last, she was free to go to the can patch. Brother Fowler and Cephas were already in the patch cutting down the sturdy dark red cane with their hoes. As it fell, Brother Ellis followed along and cut the leafy green top portion of the stalk away. This was what Papa had meant by "topping" it. Eunice joined Boland who was stripping the cane of any remaining husks.

"No need to load and haul all this waste," Bo commented as he stripped briskly. Eunice knew he was imitating Papa who had been along and said just that before she arrived. Papa's recent inspection also explained Bo's uncommon helpfulness.

On and on they worked, interrupted only by dinner. This was one day Brother Ellis couldn't linger around Midnight. It grew hot in the afternoon as they were stacking the cane in piles. The heat accentuated the fragrance of the cane, and it also lured the boys to pause to cut off a joint, peel it, and chew the sweet juice from the pulp.

Felix came riding into the patch standing up in a wagon. The boys helped him load the cane, and off he slowly bumped across the rows toward the molasses mill. By supper time he had hauled enough cane to start the mill the next morning.

Brother Bunyan spent the day chopping and hauling wood to the mill. He was to be in charge of building a crackling fire and keeping it going to cook the molasses.

But it was the actual day that the mill ran that Eunice liked. Next morning she sped madly through her chores. She threw the feed in the chicken yard so abruptly that she startled the biddies and the roosters. They cackled and cheeped in alarm. She almost turned her churn over twice. Sister Mary envisioned mopping up a whole churn full of milk and said, "Run on, Eunice. I'll finish it for you." Eunice and Bo did run. They sped across the fields, leaping over the big rows. Lucy scampered along behind them.

"Uh. Huh. Hey-o, Eunice! Hey-o, Boland!," Mr. Walker greeted them in his high-pitched voice. He and Papa already had the mill operating when they reached it. Mr. Walker and his grandson, Frank, always helped them make molasses. In turn Papa let him use the mill and helped him make his.

A mule was hitched to the long log which served as a lever. As the mule pulled the log around in a circle, Mr. Walker fed one or two stalks of cane at a time into the rollers which crushed the juice from them. The lemonade-colored juice ran down from the mill through a straining cloth into a barrel. From this barrel a pipe ran downhill under the ground to a spot twenty feet away where it emptied into another barrel, also with a strainer cloth. This barrel had a faucet so that the juice that left it could be controlled. Down, down poured the juice, as the mule plodded 'round and 'round, pulling that long log.

Impulsively, Mr. Walker picked up a little board. With a few swift blows of the hammer he nailed it crosswise on the log to make a little seat. Then he nailed a stob on it for a handhold. Up in his arms he swooped Eunice and set her astride the log on the seat so that she could ride around and around. He handed her the whip with a flourish. "Miss Eunice, you make that mule keep going."

Papa eyed his delighted daughter and remonstrated. "Mr. Walker, you'll spoil that child."

"Oh, she doesn't weigh anything, Mr. Griffin. Let's let her ride."

Eunice's eyes shone, she was so proud. Who else had ever had a special riding seat built for them on a molasses mill? None of the older ones. Nobody she ever heard of. Mr. Walker had thought of this for *her*.

She cracked the whip over the mule. "Come on, Button, get moving." Around and around she rode.

Bo sat on the cane pile and peeled some for them to chew. The joints were hard to cut off, but the peeling and sectioning were easy. The first chew of each section was the best. Eunice choked on the flow of sweet juice. Her throat just didn't seem big enough for all that.

She sat majestically as she glided around. Once she had read in the *Clarke County Democrat* about a young lady in Thomasville who went to college up at The Judson and was chosen Queen of the May. Eunice was hazy as to exactly what a Queen of the May was or did, but right now she decided she knew how a queen felt. Suddenly Lucy jumped on her shoulder. She had decided to ride, too. Soon Eunice had such a sense of good fortune that she could afford to be generous. "You can ride a while if you want to, Bo. I'll peel."

Papa made a check and saw that the second barrel was more than half full of juice. He gave the order. "Now, Bunyan, you can light that fire." Brother Bunyan took pride in his fires. He had laid a masterful one of fat, well-dried pine under the long rectangular metal cooking pan which was called an evaporator. Now he lit the newspaper he had placed on the bottom beneath a layer of kindling wood. It was no time before the flames were high.

The evaporator was twelve feet long, six feet wide, and six inches deep. It was built like a maze with partitions six inches apart. The juice first entered the passages at the far left. Underneath the left side of the thin pan the hot fire raged so that the juice began to boil vigorously the moment it entered. However, there was no fire underneath the right side of the evaporator. As the juice wended its way through the passages on that side it began to cool and thicken. By the time it made its final exit into the waiting barrel the thin juice had been cooked and cooled into a thick dark syrup.

It was an exciting scene. The fire roared and spat and crackled. Smoke billowed out of the flue which ran beneath the right half of the evaporator and curved ten feet up into the air. Woodley, Papa's other field hand, used a perforated spatula to skim the foam off the boiling syrup. He saved the foam in big pans.

Sister Nora appeared. She had come to get a gallon of foam so that she could make taffy. Woodley soon filled her bucket. Nora said, "This is a-plenty for the candy. You can pile up the rest for the hogs, Woodley. Hogs have a sweet tooth, too." Woodley was the wage-hand who had his own family. Papa had built him a place down on the road toward school.

Papa was standing over the evaporator next to Woodley and used a solid spatula to help regulate the flow of the syrup. He made sure it had become the proper consistency as it reached certain points. "Every bit of this work will all be wasted if it isn't cooked exactly right."

Eunice, who was sitting on the cane pile now, happened to glance over her shoulder. She looked again. There lay Frank fast asleep. Frank was the laziest boy in Clarke County. When he was supposed to be hoeing a patch he spent more time snoozing under a tree than he did hoeing. Eunice giggled but didn't tell.

Presently Mr. Walker began fuming. "Frank is supposed to be seeing to it that there's a fresh barrel to catch the molasses as soon as a barrel is filled. Where's he gone to? *FRANK*. Oh. *FRANK*."

Frank roused. But without opening his eyes he moaned, "I'm tired, Grandpa."

"Tired? You have the easiest job here."

"Oh, Grandpa, I'm sure I was *born* tired."

The barrel catching the molasses would have spilled over if Mr. Walker himself had not run to replace it.

Brother Bunyan kept his fire roaring. His face was red from the heat. The pine burned so readily that he had to keep feeding great stacks of it into the flames.

When the mule, Button, wearied of his endless circling journey, Eunice and Bo's usual mount, Ol' Cap, was hitched up to relieve him. By keeping the mill going all day, 100 gallons of thick mahogany-colored, ribbon cane molasses was in kegs and barrels by late afternoon. The big boys loaded it on the wagon and started for the smokehouse where they stored it lined up on a long wooden bench against the wall.

Bo peered around a high stack of crushed cane and spied Frank lying in its shelter. It had been a warm day for the last of October, and he had fallen asleep again. Bo threw back his head with laughter and taunted, "Frank's asleep again! Frank's asleep again." Bo could never completely forgive Frank for echoing his crying every morning on the way to school.

As Papa and Mr. Walker and the hands shut down the mill, Mr. Walker asked, "Mr. Griffin, you ever made sorghum molasses?"

"No, sir. That stuff makes good enough fodder, but I wouldn't put the syrup on my table. Taste is too strong. I never have bothered to grow it."

"I agree with you there. No syrup in the world like this ribbon cane cooked up the right way. And don't forget: I'm looking for you and the boys to come over and help me make mine day after tomorrow."

❦ fourteen
Halloween

"Oh, Bunyan, you don't need another biscuit," groaned Sister Nora with dismay. Nora and Mary were trying to rush the family through supper so that they could clear the dining room and stove room for the Halloween taffy-pull.

"They're going to *be* here before you finish, Fowler. Hurry, please." And, sure enough, the girls were still clearing dishes off the table when the young folks began to arrive. There were the older cousins from Uncle John's family, the Day boys, and a dozen others sprinkled from all around.

The boys helped Mary and Nora build up the fire in the kitchen stove under the kettles full of molasses foam. The foam soon began to bubble. Meanwhile, the girls laid great platters out on the dining room table and buttered them well.

Sister Mary was chatting with Earl Compton when she suddenly remembered, "Oh! Mama said to be sure to add a little vinegar to the molasses foam! I forgot!" She excused herself and ran to the kitchen.

Just then Cephas came in. He singled out Eunice. "Run Eunice, yo' Mama say she want you in her room up at the house."

Eunice thought to herself, "Mama thinks I'm too little to be out here with the young folks." She knew Bo had already been sent to bed. He had peeled and chewed cane and ridden the molasses mill until he was exhausted. In any case Mary and

Nora would not have put up with him. He had embarrassed them too often in front of their beaux. Actually, Eunice could not explain how she happened to find herself still out here at this time of night.

As she sped along the long walk from the kitchen to the house, she held her breath. The lamps in the house and the dining room made the only pinpoints of light. They by no means penetrated the darkness between the two buildings.

Suddenly a shapeless white apparition jumped up from below the raised walk. A ghost! BOO.

Eunice shrieked and ran frantically on toward the house and Mama. The ghost swayed from side to side. BOO. BOO. BOO.

Just as she reached the back door, Felix shed his sheet and called, "Jes me, Miss Newnich. Jes me. Yo' Mama don't really want you." Then he laughed with derision. "Yeee Heeee Heeeee. Heee Heeee Heee."

Eunice was blind with rage. Oh, how many times Cephas and Felix had played this trick on her. With them it was Halloween and April Fool every day.

Mama and Papa were close by the lamp, Mama mending, and Papa working at his secretary. They were so used to Eunice being teased that they hardly lifted their eyes, but Papa did comment as he started a fresh page in his ledger, "High time you tricked them back, Ootchie."

Not that Papa thought for a minute that she would. Nobody thought so: Cephas and Felix, Cousin Omer, Mr. Os—all of them thought they could torment Eunice forever and watch her weep and shriek. But they had not reckoned with this Eunice who had been riding high all day.

Eunice did not say a word. She just sat in a rocking chair and rocked hard and fast. Papa was right. High time she did some tricking herself. She rocked and she thought and she figured. Lucy appeared and hopped on her shoulder, but Eunice was unaware of her. She remained deep in her thoughts until she had a whole plan worked out in her mind.

In an *Atlanta Journal* there had been a picture of a jack-o'-lantern, and she was figuring out a way to copy it. She had never seen one in her life, and she felt sure that Felix had never seen nor heard of one.

"Mama, may I have a snip off that red lawn in your scrap box?" Eunice was already burrowing for it. "Papa, please lend me your pocket knife," she called as she scurried out to the girls' shed room to fetch her own wee brass lamp.

Equipped with the piece of red lawn, Papa's knife, and the lamp, she sneaked out to the barn where Papa stored his pumpkins. The merrymakers in the dining room were noisy indeed. Nobody else was outside: Cephas, Felix, and Fowler were watching the fun from the kitchen.

Eunice selected a choice pumpkin and rolled it out on a grassy spot behind the barn. With the light of her lamp she cleaned out the pumpkin and cut the eyes, nose, and mouth like the one in the picture in the newspaper.

The little log house where Cephas and Felix slept was built near the kitchen. Eunice sometimes rolled, sometimes carried the big pumpkin until she finally succeeded in getting it inside the little house. She put it in the corner far from the door and laid the red lawn inside over the openings. Then she set her tiny brass lamp down inside the jack-o'-lantern.

Oh, what a frightening one it was! The blood red eyes, nose, and jagged mouth leered out of the grotesque giant head. She took one last look and then went skipping back up to the dining room to see how the candy was coming along.

By this time everyone had buttered his fingers and was pulling the great golden ropes of taffy. The group had paired off into couples, and those who were sweethearts were pulling it back and forth, back and forth, looking into each other's eyes and making it last as long as possible. Sister Nora and Sister Mary were not the only ones flirting, so were Brother Bunyan and Brother Ellis. Ah hah. This would be something to mention the next time the big boys teased her.

Felix didn't have the patience to pull his piece of taffy. He snatched the dark, thin, snaky-looking strip off the platter the moment it was cool enough to touch. Then he rammed it all into his mouth and sauntered down the kitchen steps to go to his house to bed.

He opened the door and spied the jack-o'-lantern. "Yaaaaaaaaaaahhh," he screamed. "The devil's in our house! The devil's in our house!" Never had that peaceful countryside been filled with such wild and hideous screeches.

The taffy-makers rushed out to the gallery along the front of the dining room. Eunice was in the front row. She hopped up and down with glee as they all watched Felix leap over the picket fence and run down the public road half mad with terror.

Brother Bunyan dashed down the kitchen steps toward Felix's house. Sister Mary called, "Bunyan! Watch out! No telling what's in there!" The others on the porch stirred restlessly. But Bunyan went right on to the doorstep. He threw back his head and laughed when he looked inside the little house and saw what had frightened Felix. Without a word he ran in and snatched it up.

He brought the pumpkin head up the steps to the dining room and with a grand gesture set it right in the middle of the mantelpiece over the fireplace. "Who in the world made it?" he shouted.

Eunice was giddy with success. She spoke right out. "I did. That's my little brass lamp down in it, see? I'm tired of Felix playing tricks on me."

The young folks all just looked at each other, and for a few moments nobody said a word. What had come over Eunice? This was not like her.

The jack-o'-lantern, now sallow without the lamp lit inside, looked down on the family at breakfast the next morning. The buttered biscuits, grits, and ham on Eunice's plate were getting cold. Felix still hadn't come home, and somehow her victory had lost its glitter. Where was he? Off somewhere cold and trembling and crying and hungry? She wished she had not done it.

Sister Mary rose to get another pan of hot biscuits and glanced out of the window into the gray dawn. "Here he comes! Here he comes!" Eunice stood up so as to be able to see for herself.

Cephas opened the door for him, saying, "Come in here, boy! Where you been all night?"

Eunice's voice was choked with feeling. "Oh, Felix, I didn't mean to scare you *that* bad. Look up there on the mantel. Nothing but a pumpkin."

"Ho. *That*? What you talking bout? Pumpkin nuthin! Whoooooooeeeeeeee! Folks, what I seen was the devil with hell fire a-shimmerin' and a-spurtin' out from him. Big red eyes lookin' out fire. Big red nose breathin' out fire. Jagged teeth a-spittin' out fire. All red hot, I mean."

He swelled up proudly. "What I tell you is that *I* am the one 'round this place who have seen the devil."

❦ fifteen
Eunice Grows Up

Such a hard early December they had never seen. Cold rains fell and froze. "Enough to make us all sick."

Then there came a great gale. Every loose thing on the farm blew away. Mama threw up her hands in dismay. "Even the washboard's gone! Whoever heard of such winds this time of year? Must have been a tornado somewhere."

It was no big surprise when Mr. Jarvis stopped by to report that most of the roof had been blown off Eddie Megginson's barn. Eddie Megginson was Sister Maggie's husband!

Papa was quick to volunteer help for Maggie. "Cephas, you're the best carpenter on this place. Take Felix along to help you and go over and help Maggie and Eddie patch up that barn. They can't afford to lose any more fodder, and the animals will freeze out in this weather."

Then one morning Woodley came up and begged off because his wife, Cebelle, had the grippe. The next day one of their children came and rapped on the kitchen door to report, "Our Papa, he sick, too."

Mama was concerned. Papa sighed. "Did you ever? Trouble always comes double. Not a hand left to do a thing. And Midnight's foal due any time now."

But even that was not all. Just at bedtime Brother Nap rode over from Campbell with the news that Grandpa Griffin was dead. Grandpa's thin little ray of life seemed to have just flickered out in the bitter cold of this gray month.

Eunice could not believe it. She knew that some day somebody in the family would die, but this was the first time within her memory that it had happened. It was not real.

Poor Papa. He and Brother Nap agreed that the funeral had best be held the next afternoon. Of all times for Grandpa to die. Just when Midnight's foal was due.

Nobody went to bed. The entire farm was a turmoil of preparation. Sister Mary and Sister Nora owned few black clothes, and they began emptying trunks to see what they could find. The flatirons were placed by the fire so that Papa's and the boys' black trousers could be pressed, as well as skirts for Mama and the girls. Shapeless old black hats had to be stuffed with paper and steamed. Nora fussed, "Hard enough to work on black things in daytime. Terrible by lamplight."

Papa and Mama conferred and decided that Brother Ellis would stay at home to attend to milking the cows and feeding and watering the animals, and that Eunice was old enough to help him. She was to keep the fires going, feed the chickens, churn, and warm up food for Ellis. Not a word was said aloud, but everybody knew that Ellis was chosen to stay because he was best at handling Midnight. "People will never understand the entire family not being at the funeral, but what else can we do?"

The whole family was up hours before daylight. Dressing and cooking and eating breakfast and packing a lunch were going on all at once. Mama said, "Sorry to take the last cake and pie in the house, Eunice, but this was so unexpected. Can't go in on Arco without taking something."

Papa stopped Fowler from hitching up the buggy. "The mud is too deep for the buggy, Fowler. Would just tear it to pieces. We'd do better to take the two wagons."

Now Mama put on her heaviest cape and joined the others outside. She went around thrusting her hand inside each one's cloak and pinching to make sure each was warmly enough dressed. When she was satisfied that there were enough blankets and lanterns and hot bricks in the first wagon, off the older boys and girls rode. Then as she and Papa, Boland, and Fowler set out behind them, Papa reminded Ellis once more, "Now, just you see to it that Midnight stays in the stall. Keep her warm. That way I'm sure things will be all right."

It was still so dark that the family was soon out of sight. Ellis went out to the barn to milk the six cows, and Eunice headed for the chicken yard. She had fed and watered the chickens and taken the eggs into the kitchen when Ellis came in looking unhappy. "Eunice, you come milk. Midnight seems a little uneasy."

Eunice knew how to milk. She had done it many a time. But she had rarely kept at it long because someone older usually impatiently interrupted her, saying, "You run along now, Eunice, and I'll finish."

Today she finished not one cow but six. Papa didn't have any fine Jersey cows. Just scrubs. Oh, but they were hard to milk. She squeezed and pulled and squeezed and pulled. Such a weak little trickle. She wished her hands were bigger and stronger. Never again would she beg anybody to let her milk. Well. This much would just have to do. Oh, my. She sighed to think that doubtless she would have to repeat the chore before night. She worked hard, but the clock struck 11:30 before she had time to finish it. Then the churning. She must stop and warm up leftovers for their dinner.

But when Ellis came in at noon he was too upset about Midnight to eat much. "Don't take on so, Brother Ellis. Papa *had* to go to Grandpa Griffin's funeral. You know that. And you're good with horses. You know you are. Besides, we can get Mr. Jarvis if we need him."

"If everything's all right, fine," said Ellis. "But I wouldn't know what to do if anything went wrong. Oh, Eunice, you just don't know how Papa is about Midnight." But Eunice did know. Midnight represented Papa's every earthly weakness. Papa realized it, too. He hadn't named that horse for any preacher. He felt too guilty. With the money she had cost, he could have bought some good Jersey cows as well as a plenty good enough horse.

Brother Ellis grew even more fretful and gloomy as the afternoon wore on. He came in and paced up and down. "Midnight is so uneasy."

Eunice could stand it no longer. "All right. You'd feel better if Mr. Jarvis came. I'd feel better. Why don't you go on and get him or go find somebody else to go for him?"

"No use hunting somebody else. I could get to Mr. Jarvis's myself time it would take me to get one of the Walkers there. Mr. Walker's getting so old, and you know that pokey Frank."

"Ellis, the others have gone off and left us nothing but mules. It'd take you forever to get there. Wouldn't it be worth trying Mr. Williams?"

"Eunice, you know I could get there myself as soon as I could find him and get him going. Only thing is *you*. I'd get to Mr. Jarvis quicker, but I'd be gone longer from you if I go myself. Why, Eunice, you realize you'd be left here all alone."

Eunice surprised herself by shrugging her shoulders. "Pshaw. You've said yourself many a time that nobody'd have me. Besides, Woodley's house is not far."

"Eunice! Don't you dare go down there and catch the grippe!"

"I didn't say I was. Now, you go on. It's after four o'clock now. Here, I'll get your cap and cloak and gloves."Eunice warmed his heavy cloak before the fire and hastened Ellis into it. He quickly bridled a mule and rode off, goading the mule and pleading with him to move faster.

Eunice banked the fires and started right then on the night chores. She found the animals all scritched up in the corners of the buildings trying to keep warm. Better get the milking done now. She led the cows into the barn and began. Well, as long as she had to milk, she would do a good job of it. Zing. Zing. Zing. She liked to hear the first streams of milk hit the bottom of the bucket. Sounded as if you were getting a lot.

When she had taken the three gallons of milk inside, she fed and watered all the animals and fowl. There were the turkeys, the chickens, the geese, the ducks, the guineas, the hogs, the cows, the sheep, and the remaining mules. She fed sweet potatoes to the hogs and cows. Papa had so many this year that he was trying to get rid of them. Her hands grew cold, cold. Once she stopped and ran in to the fire long enough to warm them.

It was dark by the time she fed all the animals and went into Mama and Papa's room to check the fire. The funeral was no doubt over now. Everybody in the family except her would be out in the icy night. The family probably would go from the graveyard back to Brother Nap's and Bud's houses for supper before setting out on the ten-mile ride back home on the muddy road. She shivered at the thought and held out her hands gratefully toward the fire. It was such a relief to be inside that she could not feel sorry for herself being left alone.

So different it was now from the usual din. The only sounds were the logs shifting as they burned, the tick-tock of the clock, and the wind-made outside noises. She could never feel insecure in this great old room she loved so well. The original log walls inside the frame ones made it feel snug indeed compared with the rest of the house.

Should she let the fire die down some and take a lantern and go out and see about Midnight? Brother Ellis had told her that he didn't believe there was anything she could do, but it would be a relief to be sure of it.

But just then she thought she heard someone calling. Oh, no. Couldn't be. Then she heard the call again. Oh, maybe it was just the wind. No. That was surely a human voice. Major began barking. She threw her cloak around her shoulders and picked up the lamp. When she unlatched the front door, she could see two men on horses out in the public road. Why hadn't one of the riders come to the door and knocked?

"Mr. Griffin! Mr. Griffin!"

She shouted to be heard above the wind. "Mr. Griffin's not here right now. Who is it?"

"Sheriff DeLoach and a prisoner. Can we spend the night?"

There was no question in Eunice's mind. It was a Christian's duty never to turn anyone away. But a prisoner! She was used to the continuous stream of peddlers, agents, salesmen, drummers, relatives, friends of relatives, and The Law. But never before had The Law had a prisoner!

Even so it was second nature for Eunice to reply, "Hush, Major! Hush, Major! Go back under the house. Yes, Sheriff, you just come right in and we'll make home-folks of you." That was what Papa always said.

"I'll just tie the horses to the fence post here until someone can take them out to the stalls, " said the Sheriff.

Eunice was speechless now. She watched as the Sheriff ordered his handcuffed prisoner to dismount and precede him up the walk. She stepped well behind the door as she opened it, still holding the lamp aloft. "Go right on up to the fire," she motioned.

The Sheriff burst in eagerly. "A fire is what I've been dreaming of. Answer to prayer on a night like this." But no sooner had he held out his hands toward the cheerful flames than he wheeled around, saying anxiously, "But where is everybody? I don't hear a sound."

Eunice looked askance at the handcuffed prisoner. She spoke hesitantly, "Brother Ellis has gone to get Mr. Jarvis to come look at our horse."

"Yes. Brother Ellis. But I mean the rest of the family."

"Grandpa Griffin died. The funeral was today."

"Old Mr. Griffin. Too bad. God give him rest. But that means . . . Say do you mean that you're here *alone*?"

She might as well go ahead and admit it. "Well, right now I am."

"Good Lord! Oh, now. In that case we'll go on and try the next place. I stopped because we've been on the road in the cold since this morning and can't possibly make it to the Grove Hill jail tonight. Your Papa's always so nice, and your Mama always has so much good to eat . . ." He paused lamely. It was plain that the Sheriff had been living for this meal.

Eunice knew Mama and Papa would never let anybody leave hungry. That would be unthinkable. "Oh, you haven't eaten, sir! Well, I was just about to fix some supper. I can fix fried ham and rice and gravy and biscuits, and there are leftover collards. And there's lots of milk."

"Young lady, can you do that? I'd be eternally grateful."

Eunice picked up the lamp and led the two men out to the dining room. There was enough fire left in the stove so that she could get a fresh one going in a few minutes. She had watched the grown-ups boil and rinse rice too many times not to know how. And how many times she had seen Mama make biscuits! Three times a day the year round. She drew forth the big wooden bowl and made a ring of flour around the center. In the middle she worked in a handful of lard, added a pinch of soda, a dash of salt, and then poured in buttermilk a little at a time until the dough felt just right to pinch off into biscuits.

But they didn't pinch off for Eunice the way they did for Mama. Some were thin and some were fat and none was exactly round. But she did come out with some about the same as Mama: four big pans full. Oh well. Toasted leftovers would always do for breakfast. While the biscuits baked she sliced ham and put it in the skillet. Her ham slices were ragged compared to Mama's, but that wouldn't affect the taste.

It was hard to do around with the men watching her and waiting. If only they would talk or read or even just look out the window. But, no. Sheriff DeLoach just sat there with both his hands in his lap and devoted his full attention to an impatient wait. The prisoner bore no expression. He seemed numb. Eunice somehow finally had everything ready.

The Sheriff ate as if he were starved. Eunice began to wonder if he would leave enough for the prisoner. To help fill out the meal, she rose hastily and began ladling preserves out of the churns. Maybe the sweetness would help kill his appetite. She poured his glass full of milk for the third time. Too bad Mama had gone off with all the cake and pie.

But the Sheriff seemed very content to polish off his supper with the buttered biscuits and a bowl of the peach preserves. "Miss Eunice, ever who taught you to make biscuits really did a good job." Then he pushed back his chair and unlocked the hand-cuffs on the prisoner. "I guess we'll have to feed this scoundrel the scraps."

As the man ate, the Sheriff kept his hand on his pistol. Eunice wondered what the prisoner's crime had been but did not dare ask. When he, too, seemed to be finished, Eunice led the Sheriff back to Mama's room. There were no rockers out in the dining room. Then she politely inquired, "What about your horses, sir?"

"Thirsty and hungry. Your brother won't be back for awhile yet, will he? And when he does get here, he'll have himself to feed and that horse to worry with. Tell you what, Miss Eunice, I'll just chain this man to the bedstead here and leave the pistol with you while I go out and see to them."

Mr. DeLoach calmly began attaching the chain to the bedpost. He seemed unaware of Eunice's terror. She volunteered, "I know how to feed horses. I know just where the feed is. Let *me* do *that*."

"That's mighty nice of you, little lady, but you couldn't lead my horse. In fact, he wouldn't let a little girl like you get near him. He's a one-man horse if there ever was one. Don't know what would become of him if I ever got too sick to take care of him. He is especially skittish when he sees a woman. Can't stand a skirt. No, I'll go and you stand guard over this man. He can't do a thing. See—he's handcuffed, and I've chained him, and I'll leave you the pistol for good measure." As he handed it to her he nodded his head, "You're a boy now, Miss Eunice."

The Sheriff left. Eunice looked with dismay at the pistol in her hand. Never in her life had she so much as touched a firearm. She held it with the distaste she usually reserved for snakes. Then she looked at the wooden bedpost to which the prisoner was chained. My, but it looked frail and flimsy now.

The prisoner had worn the same sullen and unfeeling expression during his entire stay, but now he could not completely suppress his mirth at Eunice's obvious reaction to her assignment. What a ridiculous way for a Sheriff to handle things.

The laughter in his eyes threw panic into Eunice. She, too, thought it ridiculous of the Sheriff. Goodness. He seemed to think that just because she could make biscuits and turn out a supper, she could do anything. She'd like to fling the pistol down and run out of here like the wind. Why should she stay in here with this wicked man? She knew a hundred hiding places where nobody'd ever find her. She wished she were up underneath the house behind a chimney or, better, cozy and snug under all the hay out in the barn. Besides, the Sheriff had no right whatsoever to expect her to do such a thing for him. She was a girl, and girls were not supposed to have to hold guns and guard prisoners.

Then a picture of Grandma Holland flashed into her mind. Grandma majestically taking down that rifle and marching out to shoot any intruder. Grandma would stand right up to this man. She would not let him cow her. Grandma would say that Eunice could hold her own. After all, she had the gun.

The prisoner wasted no time in making up his mind to break loose and escape. It would be absurd to pass up the opportunity. He was well fed and rested, and nothing to stop him but a bedpost and a tiny, frightened girl. He gave her another amused glance as he pulled the chain taut to examine it.

But this time Eunice looked back at him and narrowed her eyes. She firmly put down first one foot, then the other, and stood up just as straight as Grandma Holland ever had. She continued to eye him coolly. The man sensed the difference in her and was puzzled. Eunice could tell it and continued to gain strength. What about Grandpa Griffin's mama? Husband killed by the Creeks and her stranded on the riverbank without even quilts and food for her wailing babies. She'd think a great-granddaughter of hers could at least hold a gun on a man who was chained and handcuffed. She wouldn't think this was any tight spot at all by comparison.

By now the prisoner had decided his best chance was simply to break the wooden bedpost. It was not the square and solid type. It was merely a simple carved one, and should prove no task at all for a strong man. He suddenly lunged against the chain with all his might. The bed slid, but it was made of solid walnut, and the post held. Fortunately, Eunice had kept herself at enough distance. Now, she stepped back and gave herself even more.

Up until this point she had merely been summoning enough courage to continue to hold the pistol and stay in the room with the man. Now for the first time the thought came to her that she might even have to use the gun.

The prisoner tried another attack on the post. He began to hack at it with the center of the handcuffs. The first blow mutilated the post, but it held. He gave it another blow. Another.

Eunice watched with horror. If she screamed could she be heard above the wind? Should she try to run for the Sheriff? That would be best, but she was near the fireplace, and the bed and prisoner were between her and the door. Well, should she just shut her eyes and pull the trigger? Perhaps, but she didn't want to kill anybody, and if she didn't kill him, he might be angry enough to drag the bed over to her and attack her.

Now the prisoner realized that the bedpost was deceptively strong, and he raged into it with his full might. As he drew back for another stroke, he heard an even cool voice, "You try that one more time and I'll pull this trigger. I mean it."

The man straightened in surprise and turned to look at her. He could not believe his ears. The little girl standing there was not at all the same one the Sheriff had left. He had had no reason whatever to expect opposition from the little girl the Sheriff had left. This one was not the same. Same dress, but not at all the one who was there minutes before.

He was no more surprised than was Eunice. She was amazed at how it felt to be like Grandma Holland and Grandma Griffin. She repeated determinedly, "I mean it. I'll shoot. And everybody says I have very good aim. You hear?"

The man was still staring at her numbly when the door flew open. Sheriff DeLoach strode in. He snatched the pistol from Eunice and brandished it at the man. "Get back there! Get back there this minute, you . . ."

The prisoner stepped back obediently. He then slumped to the floor, immediately resuming the resigned, dull expression he had worn before Eunice had been left in charge.

Still holding the gun carefully, the Sheriff edged back toward the fireside, twirled a straight chair around to face the prisoner, and seated himself, sighing, "Now then."

He was all contrition. To Eunice he said, "Little lady, I apologize. That was a fool stunt I did, leaving you. I was worried so about those horses that I wasn't using my head. Too tired to be sensible. Too long a day. Just not thinking. This man's been so worn out himself ever since I took him in tow that I was thrown off my guard. I'll never forgive myself for being such a fool, though, considering the record he's got. From here on out I'm holding a gun on him every minute. When your folks get here, your Papa and brothers can spell me long enough to get a little sleep."

Forty-five minutes later Brother Ellis and Mr. Jarvis were back. Brother Ellis roared from the yard, "Eunice, we're here. We're going straight on out to the barn. Make something hot to drink and have it ready for us. I'll be back for it."

She went out to the kitchen building to boil coffee. Ellis soon came to fetch it. He reported, "Mr. Jarvis says Midnight is all right. But he says we may as well just lie down in the stall next to hers and be there if we're needed. He says to leave enough hot coals in the stove to keep some water warm."

Eunice didn't even tell him about the Sheriff and the prisoner up in the house. No need to bother him or take his time. Ellis had not seen the two extra horses. Midnight was in the barn beyond the garden, and the Sheriff was used to putting his horse in the stalls on the other side of the road.

When the family drove up way late in the night, they were bewildered. Mama exclaimed as Eunice ran to the door to meet them, "Child! Mercy day! What are you doing up? I expected you to be asleep! Where is Ellis? Something wrong with Midnight?" Suddenly she perceived the Sheriff. "Why, good evening, Sheriff!" Then she caught sight of the gun and the prisoner. She shrank back. "What in the world is going on here? Who is this man?"

Papa's eyes repeated Mama's questions. Eunice began explaining, "Ellis is down in the barn. And Mr. Jarvis is with him just to make sure everything is all right. No, Papa. No foal yet."

Sheriff DeLoach interrupted. He couldn't wait to tell all that had happened. He described how smoothly he had found the farm running and the supper Eunice had prepared. Then he spared no details in his account of how she had guarded, defied, and threatened the prisoner. The hacked and battered bedpost offered mute testimony. Brother Bunyan and Brother Fowler stared at each other and turned to look at her as Mr. DeLoach concluded, "Yes, indeed, Mr. Griffin. I have never had a better deputy than your daughter, Eunice. Spunkier than most men would have been."

The next morning Papa, Mr. Jarvis, and Ellis were late coming to the breakfast table. They were all exuberant. Midnight's foal was here! "Oh, but he's a beauty. Black like Midnight but with a ring of white just above each hoof."

Mr. Jarvis just kept saying over and over, "Quality. Quality. Quality. Yes, that little fellow is going to be worth something. Valuable. Very valuable." Mr. Jarvis' conscience had always bothered him about encouraging Papa to buy a horse he knew was beyond his means. Now he felt relieved.

None of the Griffins wanted to eat. They would have liked to push back the benches from the table and run to the barn. But they had to restrain themselves and somehow wade through the big breakfast in front of them. The Sheriff alone enjoyed it. He paused only long enough to wave a biscuit and shout, "It's good, Miss Eunice, but not a bit better 'n yours."

Papa was not eating with the family. He was guarding the prisoner. Without turning his eyes from the man, he asked in an even voice, "Well, Deputy Eunice, how about you naming this foal? What shall we call him?"

Eunice could not believe her ears. The whole family, Mr.

Jarvis, and Sheriff DeLoach there, and here was Papa singling her out. "Oh, Papa!" She looked all around the table as she searched her thoughts for a name. But she stopped when her eyes met Brother Ellis's.

She had always resented and envied Ellis's privileges with Midnight. She knew the other boys thought Papa was showing him undue partiality even though he was the eldest boy still at home. But after yesterday she no longer felt that way at all. Ellis had earned his right to ride Midnight. He had never joined his brothers on fishing trips or sitting around the warm fire in bad weather until he had tended her. Papa had to remind the other boys to do their work. Ellis never had to be prodded.

Eunice said firmly, "Brother Ellis deserves to name him."

"Well! You have a name, Ellis?"

Ellis had already thought of one. Of course he had. It was a good Bible name to please Papa. "Jeremiah. And we can call him Jerry for short."

The Sheriff must have stopped and told everybody on the way to Grove Hill about Eunice and the prisoner. Her brothers told it at Day's store. The news spread.

On the day after the funeral all the Griffin children stayed home from school out of respect for Grandpa, but on the following day they met the Days outside and joined them as usual. But this time the older Days didn't immediately go on ahead and leave her behind with Alice and Boland. Instead, they lingered to ask Eunice questions about her exciting adventure. And this time, as the group arrived in the clearing around the schoolhouse, Cousin Omer bobbed out of nowhere and leapt into the air with his salutation. "Hooooooo-eeeeeeee!

Eunice! From now on when *you* say 'frog',folks are going to hop." Not one single time that day did Cousin Omer so much as pull her braids.

Furthermore, the next day when they came home from school, Mama sang out, "It's high time we start the Christmas baking. Come on now, girls, I need you, too. Let's see, Mary. Was it you who wanted to try your hand at pound cake this time? And, Nora. Do you still want to make a marble cake? Eunice, what about you? High time you were learning to stir up a cake." Listen to this. Mama was going to let her cook. Not just run for the eggs and flour the raisins but really make a whole cake all by herself.

Now Mama asking her, "What kind do you want it to be, Eunice?"

There was no question in her mind. "Molasses cake. By Grandma's recipe."

Mama stepped to the kitchen door and called, "Boland! Run here, Boland! We need you to run to the smokehouse and fill the molasses pitchers." Boland looked puzzled. That was Eunice's job.

Mama explained, "Eunice is going to be busy putting together a cake. We're starting the Christmas baking."

At that Boland cheered. "Cake! Hooray! Will you let me lick the bowl, Sister Eunice?"

Eunice stood still a moment and closed her eyes. She wanted to hear Bo's words again in her mind. Yes, it was true. Bo had just called her Sister Eunice.

Historical Note

Eunice Griffin was born on the farm near Elam Church in Clarke County, Alabama, which is the site of this book, on December 20, 1882. She married George Bryant White on December 20, 1903, at Campbell, Alabama. They lived in Thomasville for a few years, where their first child, Annie Louise, was born in 1905. Shortly thereafter the family moved to Aliceville, Alabama, where seven more children were born, including Mary Kathleen, the author of this book, who was born on July 17, 1917. In 1924 the White family moved to Canton, Mississippi, where Eunice resided with her family at 410 (renumbered 437) South Liberty Street until her death on December 21, 1961, just one day after celebrating her seventy-ninth birthday. She was survived by seven of her children and seven grandchildren and is buried in the Canton cemetery with her husband.

This book is a fictionalized account of events that took place during Eunice's eleventh to fourteenth years, based on her recollections as told to her daughter, Kay, many years later.

T.S.

Printed by McNaughton & Gunn, Ann Arbor, Michigan